Short Stories About Numbers

Rajnish Kumar

Universities Press

Short Stories about Numbers

UNIVERSITIES PRESS (INDIA) PRIVATE LIMITED

Registered Office
3-6-747/1/A and 3-6-754/1, Himayatnagar,
Hyderabad 500 029 Telangana, India
E-mail: info@universitiespress.com

Distributed by
Orient Blackswan Private Limited

Registered Office
3-6-752, Himayatnagar, Hyderabad 500 029 Telangana, India

Other Offices
Bengaluru, Bhopal, Chennai, Guwahati,
Hyderabad, Jaipur, Kolkata, Lucknow, Mumbai,
New Delhi, Noida, Patna, Vijayawada

First Published 2010
Reprinted 2017

ISBN: 978 81 7371 698 0

Typeset at Revival 565BT 10/12 *by*
OSDATA, Hyderabad 500 049

Printed at
Charita Impressions
Hyderabad

Published by
Universities Press (India) Private Limited
3-6-747/1/A and 3-6-754/1, Himayatnagar, Hyderabad 500 029, Telangana, India
E-mail: info@universitiespress.com

Contents

Preface

God created the integers, all the rest is the work of man

Mathematics is embedded in the structure of the universe. Although mathematical systems are uninhibited inventions of the human mind, they have the astonishing ability to explain many mysterious phenomena of nature. Eugene Wigner, the great mathematician was prompted to call this remarkable ability, the 'unreasonable effectiveness of mathematics'.

In fact, many areas of mathematics have begun as a solution to real world problems. Algebra originated to solve problems in arithmetic. Geometry has its origin in calculation of distances, angles and areas. Statistics has its origin in gambling and the calculation of the probability of winning in a game of chance.

In order to have wider applications, mathematics involves abstraction, a process of generalising the essence of a mathematical concept and removing all dependence on the real world problem. Abstraction reveals deep connections between different areas of mathematics but has the disadvantage that highly abstract concepts are more difficult to learn.

Abstraction and the pedagogical method of teaching mathematics turn away the not so ambitious student from pursuing mathematics as a career. Mathematics is taught from a structural or application point of view, its tools built up in a rigorously logical, sequential way, smaller pieces fitting accurately to larger blocks. This is the main reason why most students, after 12 years of schooling, think that mathematics is a pointless exercise, and its application to real life amounts to the addition needed in totalling the grocery bill.

Yet mathematics has its fans—something in its innate quality fascinates a certain bend of mind, not just professionals but amateurs too. Amateurs, belonging to diverse professions like the military and law, have 'attacked' the foundations of mathematics—found proofs to century-old problems, calculated large primes, and found the trillionth digit of π. They might not be able to surpass brilliant mathematicians, but they can certainly have exciting explorations.

This book provides a collection of off-beat, fun-filled topics—questions which may have arisen in the curious minds of all those who have had years of mathematics teaching, but whose answers are generally beyond the scope of the syllabus.

Most mothers had a tough time explaining to their child that 11 is eleven and not oneteen and 12 is twelve and not twoteen. The early learner would have often wondered why of all bases, this strange number 2.718... was chosen as the natural logarithm base called, *e*. After all, why is mathematics left out of the Nobel Prize race by the Academy? Did you know that only a few folds of a paper could take you to the moon? The binary system is alright but why does the computer use such a strange notation as AD45F3? These are just a few of the questions answered in this book.

The reader would find unbelievable things like a triangle whose angles add up to more than 180°.

Why is the taxicab number 1729 so famous? A square-tyred bicycle can move smoothly on a path—albeit a strange path. All this and many more interesting stories will be found in the book.

Short Stories about Numbers is a collection of several thoughts, articles, brilliant number sequences and puzzles. They have been collected over years of 'adventuring' in mathematics, with only a love and passion for numbers. It is not for serious mathematicians, nor for people who know too much and find the book a mere carbon copy of their own reproductions. The author claims absolutely no originality in the work.

The book should be read with a rough page and pencil—that's the only way to enjoy it.

Rajnish Kumar
rajnishkumar1971@yahoo.co.in

1

Evolution of the Notation of Numbers

NO one knows the origin of the symbols for the numbers we use today—those known as international numbers. The most commonly accepted theory is that they are of Hindu origin passed on to the Arabs during the eighth century. Because of this they are called the Hindu–Arabic numerals. It was a book written by the great Arab mathematician, Abu Ja'far Muḥammad ibn Mūsa al-Khāwarizmī (c.778–850) that greatly influenced the introduction of the Hindu–Arabic numerals to Europe. This could be the reason why it is sometimes assumed that the numerals were ideograms created by al-Khāwarizmī.

It is opined that he used the abacus notation for developing the decimal system. Incidentally, for those who are unaware—an *abacus* is a calculating device, probably of Babylonian origin, that was important for a very long period of time in commerce. It is the ancestor of the modern calculating machine and the computer. Unlike the later and more commonly known abacus which consisted of a rectangular frame with beads sliding on wires, the Babylonian abacus consisted of a board marked with lines and equipped with counters whose positions indicated numerical values—ones, tens, hundreds, and so on.

In the abacus, the numbers 1, 2, 3, 4 were defined using additive angles.

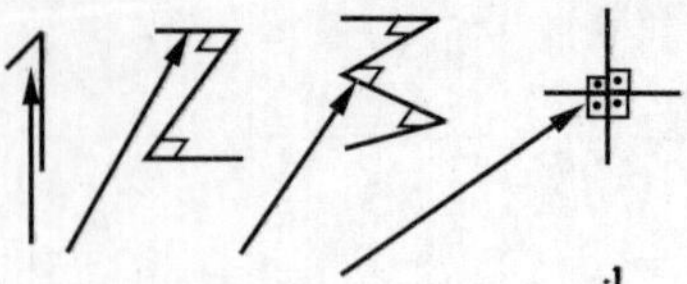

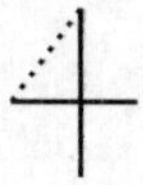

The additive angles 1,2,3 and 4 are as depicted.

Roots of the 1, 2, 3 and 4 digits

The number 1 has one angle.

The number 2 has two additives angles.

The number 3 has three additives angles.

The number 4 has four additive angles.

As can be seen from the figure, the number 4 probably got closed due to cursive handwriting.

Roots of the 5 to 10 numbers

The circle represented the hand, which has five fingers—therefore the circle represented the number 5. It was written under the line. The number 10 was placed above the line. It meant that the number on top acquired double value.

Circles, up traces, additive angles and the write line

To the circle five, if one trace up was added, with one additive angle, it made the number six.

If two up traces were added, with two additive angles, it made the number seven.

Circles, down traces, diminutive angles and the write line

To the circle ten, if one down trace was added, with one diminutive angle, it made the number nine.

If two down traces were added, with two diminutives angles, it made the number eight.

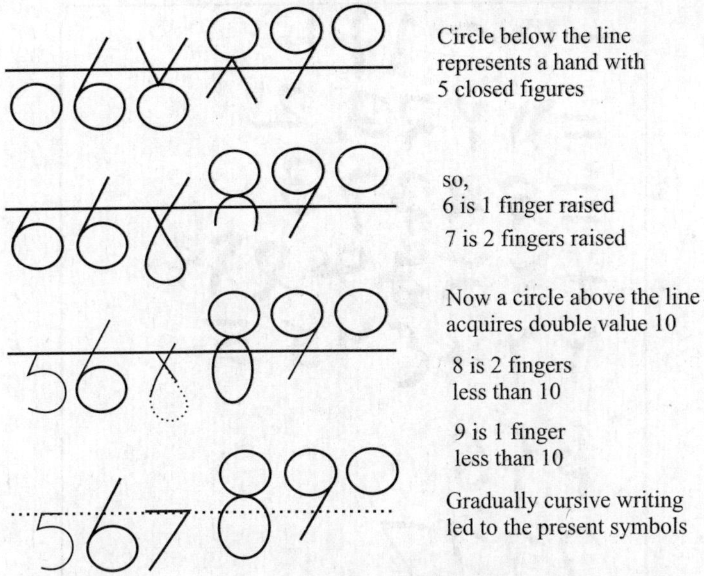

The cursive handwriting made certain changes to the crude symbols, which finally evolved to the current aesthetic format. The cursive numbers five and the number seven still use the write line on their structures.

The number seven was placed totally under the write line. It was the number that was most simplified during its cursive evolution. The involution of the number seven was necessary due to the similarities that the cursive seven had with the other numbers.

The figure given on the next page depicts another probable evolution of symbols for the numbers. It is interesting to find that the same types of symbols evolved across civilisations. Some were retained in their original form, but the Arabic system found universal acceptance and is now the international numeral system.

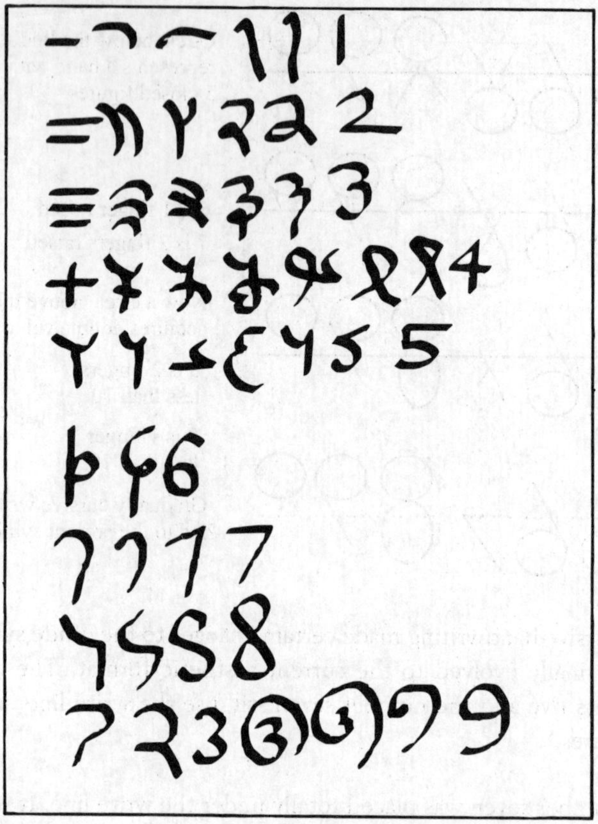

2

Origin of the Mathematical Operators, Terms and Symbols

SChool teachers often break their heads while trying to explain the significance of + − ×÷ =<> to the child. To a beginner introduced to the mysterious symbols of mathematics, all this is confusing. Gradually, though, the signs and symbols become ingrained in the memory, and all the arithmetic is quietly done. But the curious mind's journey does not end here: why do we use the sign (=) for equality and a lot more similar questions keep revolving around one's head. The evolution of a few of the most used symbols and terms has been researched and they make very interesting stories. The most important written source is the definitive *A History of Mathematical Notations* by Florian Cajori.

Symbols

Equality

The equal symbol (=) was not really in print until the early 17th century. It was previously abbreviated as *aeq*. It is contended by Cajori (Cajori, Florian. *A History of Mathematical Notation*. Macmillan. 1926) that the symbol = was developed at the University of Bologna. Robert Recorde first used the symbol in *The Whetstone of Witte* (1557), a treatise on algebra, reasoning that instead of repeating the use of the words, 'is equal to', it was more aesthetic and logical to use a pair of parallel lines—what could be more equal?

Plus and minus

The introduction of the + and – symbols can be traced back to the Germans. The *Mercantile Arithmetic* of Johannes Widmann, brought out in 1489 in Leipzig, is the earliest printed book in which the + and – symbols have been used. Widmann did not restrict the use of the + sign to ordinary addition; it had the more general meaning of 'et' or 'and' as in the heading, '*regula augmenti* + *decrementi*.' The – sign is used to indicate subtraction, but not regularly so. The word 'plus' does not occur in Widmann's text, although the word 'minus' is used two or three times. The symbols + and – were used in 1518, by Heinrich Schreiber, a teacher at the University of Vienna. Thus, gradually adoption of the + and – symbols became universal. Several independent studies of Latin manuscripts of the 14th and 15th centuries make it almost certain that the + sign comes from the Latin *et* and is merely a ligature for 'et', much in the same way that we have the ligature '&' for the word 'and'. According to Cajori, the origin of the sign – is uncertain. It may have emanated from the habit of early scribes who used it as a shorthand equivalent of 'm' for 'minus'.

The first one to make use of these signs in writing an algebraic expression was the Dutch mathematician Vander Hoecke. The symbols seem to have been employed for the first time in arithmetic by Georg Walckl in 1536. Most of the English writers of this period reserved the + and – signs as symbols of operation for algebra. Robert Recorde used it in his 1557 book, *The Whetstone of Witte*.

Division

There are several different symbols associated with the division operation like $\overline{)}$, /, :, and ÷. We will discuss the origin of the ÷ symbol called an *obelus*. Although the division sign ÷ was first used in England and America in the 17th century, it had long been used on the continent of Europe to indicate subtraction. Like most elementary combinations of lines and points, the symbol is old.

It was used as early as the 10th century for the word *est* which roughly means 'is'. When written after the letter 'i', it symbolised *id est* which means 'that is to say'. When written after the word 'it', it symbolised 'interest.' It is possible that it denoted division when written after the word *divisa*, for *divisa est*. Thus, the usage of the symbol was not unique—for example, 15th century Lombard merchants used it to indicate half. It was first completely used for a division symbol around 1650. There is also some evidence that some Italian algebraists used it to indicate division, for example in the manuscript entitled *Arithmetica and Practtica* by Giacomo Filippo Biodi dal Aucisco in 1684.

Multiplication

William Oughtred (1574–1660) contributed vastly to the propagation of mathematical knowledge in English by his treatises, *Clavis Mathematicae* (1631), published in Latin (English edition, *The Key to Mathematics*, 1647), *Circles of Proportion* (1632), and *Trigonometrie* (1657). Oughtred laid extraordinary emphasis upon the use of mathematical symbols—altogether he used over 150 of them. Three have survived to the modern times, namely the $\times$ symbol for multiplication, the :: for proportion, and the $\sim$ for 'difference between'.

Leibniz (1646–1715), though, had serious, logical doubts and reservations to the use of Oughtred's cross symbol because of the possible confusion with the letter 'x'. On July 29, 1698 he wrote in a letter to John Bernoulli, '*I do not like (the cross) as a symbol for multiplication, as it is easily confounded with x; .... often I simply relate two quantities by an interposed dot and indicate multiplication* by ZC. LM'.

Inequality

Thomas Harriot (1560–1621) was an English mathematician who lived most of his life in the sixteenth century but whose outstanding publication appeared in the seventeenth century. His great work, the *Artis Analyticae Praxis* was published in London posthumously in 1631, and deals largely with the theory of equations. In it were the symbols, ‘>’ used for ‘ is greater than’, and ‘<’ used for ‘is less than’.

The story goes that while Harriot was surveying North America, he saw a Native American with this symbol on his arm ≭. It has been conjectured that he developed the two symbols from this symbol. But it is now known that the symbols were not due to Harriot (as is often claimed), but were introduced by the editor of *Artis Analyticae Praxis*.

The symbols were not immediately accepted, for many writers preferred the symbols (shown below), which William Oughtred had suggested in the same year, in his popular *Clavis Mathematicae*, a work on arithmetic and algebra that did much towards spreading mathematical knowledge in that country.

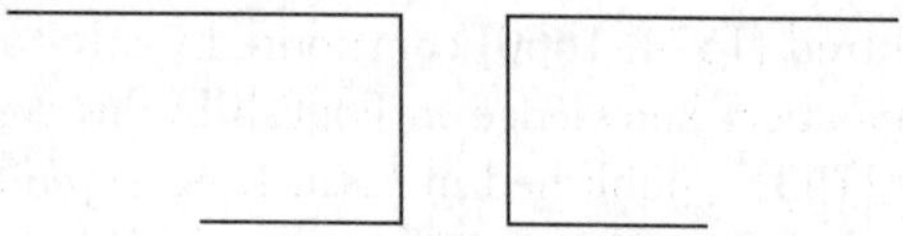

Greater than Less than

Percentage %

Percentages have been used since the end of the fifteenth century in business problems such as computing interest, profit and loss, and taxes. However, the concept of percentages had its origin much earlier. During the time of Julius Caesar, and later the Roman emperor, Augustus it was decreed that one hundredth (1/100) part of the value of all things sold at auctions had to be paid as tax (*centesima rerum venalium*). Other Roman taxes included 1/20 on every freed slave and 1/25 on every slave sold. Thus, without recognising percentages as such, the early Romans used fractions easily reduced to hundredths.

The percent sign, %, probably evolved from the symbol shown above introduced in an anonymous Italian manuscript of 1425. Instead of using ‘per 100’ or ‘per cento’ which were common at that time, this author used the symbol shown.

Terms

Addition

Fibonacci used the Latin *additio*, although he also used *compositio* and *collectio* for the operation of summing two or more numbers. The arithmetic word 'add' is from the Latin root *addere*, meaning 'to give' or 'to do'. The *dere* part of the root is the same root that gives us the word 'data/datum ' and the name for dice. Donation and condone also share the same root. The first recorded use of the word 'addition' in English is in *The Crafte of Nombrynge*. The document was one of the first English language documents dealing with mathematics.

Compute

The word is formed by joining *com* (with) and the Latin root *putare*. This root is often cited as related to thinking or reckoning, but its meaning comes from an early word for 'cut' or 'slice'. The same root appears in amputate. The word 'compute' goes back to the earliest use of numbers in commerce and the idea of comparing values to a counting or tally stick. The sticks were notched to record values for future reference. Computing then, was comparing the quantity to the marks on the tally stick.

Digit

The word 'digit' refers both to fingers (and toes) as well as the Arabic number symbols for 0 to 9. It comes from the root Indo-European word, *deik* and is related to many other words that reflect the use of the hands and fingers to 'point' out objects. Index, indicate, dictate, indict, token, dice, judge and teach are all related to the same root.

Calculate/calculus

The origin of both these words is in the Greek word *kalyx*, for 'pebble' or 'small stone'. The manipulations of small stones on counting boards to do arithmetic operations led to the present mathematical meanings of calculate and calculus. The pebble root is still present in the medical use of the word 'calculus', used to describe an accretion of mineral salts in the body into stones such as kidney stones.

Difference

It is a combination of two roots *dis* (away) and *ferre* (Latin for 'to carry'). The difference between two numbers is the amount that one has been 'carried away' from the other. Fertile comes from the same root, unlike the word 'ferry' which comes from the old-English word for 'carry'—*ferian*.

Divide

Divide shares its major root with the word 'widow'. The root *vidua* refers to a separation. A widow is one who is separated from the spouse. The prefix, *di*, of divide is a contraction of '*dis*', a two-word meaning 'apart' or 'away', as in the process of division in which equal parts are separated from each other. The *vi* part of *vidua* is also derived from a two-word, and has the same root as vigesimal (two tens), for things related to twenty. An individual is one who cannot be divided.

Arithmetic

Arithmetic was the Greek word for 'number', and is closely related to the root of 'reckon', which is an obsolete term for 'count'. In the middle ages, the best mathematicians of Germany were called *Reichenmeister* and their arithmetic texts were referred to as *Reichenbucher*. The first part of the word is drawn from the Indo-European root *ar* that is related to 'fitting together' and gives us words like army, and art. Order, adorn, and rate all come from variants of the same root.

Average

The meaning of average, as it is used in mathematics today, comes from a commercial practice of the shipping age. The root, *aver*, means 'to declare'. The shippers of goods had to declare the value of their goods. When the goods were sold, a deduction was made from each person's share, based on their declared value, for a portion of the loss—their average.

Fraction

Fraction comes from the Latin word *frangere* meaning 'to break'. A fraction represents the broken portion of a whole .

Hundred

Hundred is from the German root *hundt*. The quantity that it represents has not been consistent over the years and has ranged from its present value 100, to 112, 120, 124, and 132 at different times in different areas. The remnants of these old measures still persist in the hundredweight of some countries representing 112 or 120 pounds, depending on the country.

Multiply

Multiply comes from the combined roots of *multi* meaning 'many', and *pli*, for folds, as in a number folded on itself many times.

Thousand

Our number for one thousand comes from an extension of hundred. The roots are from the Germanic roots *teue* and *hundt*. *Teue* refers to a thickening or swelling, and *hundt* is the root of our present day 'hundred'. A thousand thus literally means a swollen or large hundred. The root *teue* is the basis of such common words today as thigh, thumb, tumour, and tuber.

3

Etymology of Algebra

THe word 'algebra' is a Latin variant of the Arabic word *al-jabr*. The word came from the title of Muhammad ibn Mūsa al-Khawarizmī's book, *Hidab al-jabr wal-muqubala*, written in Baghdad about 825 CE.

al-Khāwarizmī used the words *jabr* (JAH-ber) and *muqubalah* (moo-KAH-ba-lah) to label two basic operations used while solving equations.

The term *jabr* meaning 'restoration' was used for the operation which would transpose subtracted terms to the other side of an equation. Consider the equation

$$x - 4 = 12 \tag{1}$$

and the situation when (1) becomes

$$x = 16 \tag{2}$$

The left-side of (1), where x is lessened by 4, is *restored* or *completed* back to x in the second equation.

Muqabalah meaning 'cancellation' was used for the operation which would cancel like terms on opposite sides of an equation.

Consider the equations $x + y$ and $y + 7$. If $x + y = y + 7$, *muqabalah* gives us $x = 7$, by *cancelling* or *balancing* the two sides of the equation.

Eventually the term '*muqabalah*' was left behind, and this type of mathematics involving equations became known as '*algebra*' in many languages.

Incidentally, if we translate the title of al-Khāwarizmi's book, it would roughly read as *The Book of Completion and Cancellation* or *The Book of Restoration and Balancing.*

It is interesting to note that the word *al-jabr* used non-mathematically made its way into Europe through the Spanish Moors. Thus an *algebrista* was a bone-setter, or a '*restorer*' of bones. A barber during the medieval times called himself an algebrista since barbers often did bone-setting and bloodletting on the side. The red and white striped barber poles which exist even today, was first used to symbolise the bandages used during the bloodletting procedure: red for the blood-stained and white for the clean bandages.

The first use of the word '*algebra*' in English was by the Welsh mathematician and textbook writer, Robert Recorde in his *Pathway of Knowledge* (1551).

Algebra uses equations and variables. It is the heart of problem-solving and can be very exciting. But maybe due to its abstract nature and a lot of misrepresentation, it is one subject that all school-goers approach with fear.

4

Why is Eleven not Oneteen and Twelve not Twoteen?

CHildhood is the age of curiosity and questions. There are few mothers who have not been harried with their child's perpetual question 'why?'—more so when they need to make the child memorise things which in their adult mind are taken for granted. Take for instance the count from ten to twenty. The curious child would wonder about the oddity of 'eleven' and 'twelve'. Given that the rest of the numbers is got by adding the single digit number to 'teen' (thirteen = three + *teen* (Old English for 'ten more than'); fourteen = four + teen), the most obvious thing would be to call them *oneteen* and *twoteen*. Why, then, this strange notation?

We have ten fingers on both hands and since the most basic counting and calculation operations are done using the finger and thumb (in fact, counting started that way), it was only natural that 10 became the base for counting—the decimal system.

Eleven is a derivative of the Old English word *endleofan*. Related forms in various Germanic languages point back to the original Germanic word *ainlif* from the root *ain* meaning 'one', and the suffix *lif* from the Germanic root *lib* meaning 'remain left over.' Thus, 'eleven' literally means 'one-left over' (that is, past ten). In a similar manner, the word 'twelve' is from the Old English word *twelfe,* which could be from the Germanic word *twailif* meaning 'two-left over' (past ten).

But all this does not answer the question why eleven and twelve are termed differently from the other '*teen*' numbers. It could be the vestigial remains of the use of the duodecimal system (where 12 is the base for counting) used by many early civilisations.

The decimal system, as humanity soon found out, has a small drawback—there are not many proper factors of 10, just 2 and 5. It was felt that the duodecimal system of 12 had an advantage over the decimal system since it had 2, 3, 4 and 6 as factors. Even now, 12 being a versatile denominator in fractions may explain why we have 12 inches in a foot, 12 ounces in a troy pound, 12 old British pence in a shilling and 12 items in a dozen.

Many civilisations started using the duodecimal system. There are 12 signs of the zodiac. There are 12 hours in a day or night. All traditional Chinese calendars, clocks and compasses have their bases in 12.

Various other reasons for this use can be cited:

- 12 is the approximate number of lunar months in an Earth year;
- 12 is the sum of ten fingers on human hands and two feet; or
- 12 is the number of phalanx bones in the four fingers of one hand, with the thumb used as an indicator.

Though 12 having more factors might be a more rational reason, the last fact mentioned above seems to be the most authentic one.

Thus, the number twelve was important in ancient times. Even when the decimal system became prevalent, in many languages—in the Germanic languages at any rate—number elements were not repeated until after the number twelve. Thus the Germanic compounds *ain-lif* and *twa-lif* for eleven and twelve.

So, if you notice, some things are the way they are, not because of a rational reason but because it was traditionally so.

5

The World's Largest Number

WHat is the largest number? —a serious mathematician might consider this a too trivial question to even spend half an hour's thought on it. When everybody has spoken so much about infinity and all its related mind-boggling magnitudes, how can we possibly define the world's largest number?

But still it might be worthwhile to look at some very, very large numbers and see what they actually mean—it might bring us to a closer understanding of infinity.

Googol

When Dr Edward Kasner, an American mathematician of the early twentieth century, asked his nephews to think of a name for a 1 followed by 100 zeros, his nine-year-old nephew came up with the name 'googol'. 10^{100} is an incredibly large number. The largest reasonable estimate for the number of particles in the universe is only about 10^{85}. A googol is a million times a billion times this much!

$$\text{GOOGOL} = 10^{100}$$

The world's largest number, according to the Guinness Book of Records, is *Graham's number*. The number is named after Ronald L Graham, juggler, acrobat, and mathematician. Of course, every good mathematics student knows that there can be no 'largest' number—

what the record book actually lists is the largest number ever used in a proof. The number is incomprehensibly large, beyond images like the number of grains of sand needed to fill the universe or any such comparison. It cannot even be described with conventional numerical techniques. David Wells wrote in *The Penguin Dictionary of Curious and Interesting Numbers*, 'If all the material in the universe was turned into pen and ink it would not be enough to write the number down.' A special notation was invented by Donald Knuth, to write it down, and even then it grows out of reason . . .

Consider the number 3^3. It means '3 cubed', as it often does in computer printouts.

3^^3 means 3^(3^3), or 3^27, which is already quite large:

$3^{27} = 7,625,597,484,987...$

So,

3^^^3 = 3^^(3^^3)

= 3^^7,625,597,484,987

= 3^(7,625,597,484,987^7,625,597,484,987)

which makes a tower of exponents 7,625,597,484,987 layers high.

And 3^^^^3 = 3^^^(3^^^3), of course.

Graham's number only starts here. Consider the number 3^^^ . . .^^^ 3 in which there are 3^^^^3 carets. A largish number! Next construct the number 3^^^ . . .^^^ 3 where the number of carets is the previous 3^^^ . . .^^^ 3 number!

A *googolplex*, is a number which is impossible to write down with ordinary numeration, since this would entail the digit '1' followed by a *googol* of zeroes.

$$10^{10^{100}}$$

GOOGOLPLEX

6

Sifr: The Father of Zero

IT is widely believed that the invention of 'zero' was one of the most important events in mathematics. The word 'zero' is itself peculiar and its evolution is even more interesting. It comes from the Arabic *sifr* (صفر) meaning 'empty' or 'vacant', a literal translation of the Sanskrit word *śunya* meaning 'void' or 'empty'. Through transliteration this became *zephyr* or *zephyrus* in Latin.

In Latin *zephyrus* means 'west wind'; when used as a proper noun *Zephyrus* was the Roman god of the west wind (after the Greek god Zephyros). Since zero came to be associated with it, zephyr came to mean a light breeze— 'an *almost* nothing'. The word *zephyr* survives with this meaning in English today. The Italian mathematician Fibonacci (c.1170–1250), who grew up in Arab North Africa and is credited with introducing the Arabic decimal system to Europe, used the term *zephyrum* for what we now know as zero. This became *zefiro* in Italian, which was shortened to *zero* in the Venetian dialect, giving the modern English word.

Words derived from *sifr* and *zephyrus* gradually came to refer to calculation, as the decimal zero and its new mathematics penetrated throughout Europe. In thirteenth century Paris, a 'worthless fellow' was called a . . . *cifre en algorisme*, i.e., an 'arithmetical nothing'. (*Algorithm* is also a borrowing from the Arabs, in this case from the name of the 9th century Arab mathematician, al-Khawarizmi). This Arabic root gave rise to the modern French *chiffre*, which means digit, figure or number; *chiffrer*, to calculate or compute; and *chiffré*, encrypted; as well as to the English word '*cipher*'. Today, the word in Arabic is still *sifr*, and derivations of *sifr* are common throughout the languages of Europe. A few additional examples are:

1. **Polish**: *cyfra*, digit; *szyfrować*, to encrypt
2. **German**: *ziffer*, digit, figure, numeral, cypher
3. **French**: *zéro*, zero
4. **Spanish**: *cifra*, figure, numeral, cypher, code; *cero*, zero
5. **Swedish**: *siffra*, numeral, sum, digit

But it is strange that in Modern Greek, zero is translated as $M\eta\delta\acute{\epsilon}\nu$ (meithen), completely different from *sifr*.

Zero as a decimal digit

The earliest known *decimal digit* zero was probably introduced by Indian mathematicians sometime around the 3rd century. It was written in the shape of a dot, and consequently called *bindu* 'dot'. An early documented use of the zero by *Brahmagupta* dates to 628 CE. He treated zero as a number and discussed operations involving it. By this time (7th century), the concept had clearly reached Cambodia, and historians believe that these ideas later spread to China and the Islamic world.

The Hindu–Arabic number system reached Europe in the late 11th century. The Italian mathematician Fibonacci was instrumental in bringing the system into European mathematics around 1200 CE, though he spoke of zero as a 'sign', and not as a number.

7

Why is There no Nobel Prize in Mathematics?

THose of us who follow the announcement of the annual Nobel Prize awards for the world's most promising scientists, technologists, economists, peace brokers, may have wondered why, mathematics, which after all has served humanity in myriad ways, has been left out of the fray.

There are many stories, some strange and fantastic, to explain this omission—mainly because no official reason has been cited. One melodramatic story goes like this: the Swedish mathematician, Gosta Magnus Mittag-Leffler, had run off with Alfred Nobel's wife. If a Nobel prize for mathematics had been instituted, Mittag-Leffeler, because of his important discoveries in mathematics, would have been a prime candidate for it. So, Nobel, in revenge, refused to endow a prize for mathematics. But this story is beyond credence, as Alfred Nobel never really married. Another story leaves out the romantic angle and plainly states that Mittag-Leffler's fame and wealth antagonised Nobel.

But most scholars are of the opinion that Mittag-Leffler and Nobel had almost no relation to each other—Nobel emigrated from Sweden in 1865 when Mittag-Leffler was just a student and rarely returned to visit. Perhaps the idea for a Nobel Prize in mathematics did not occur to Alfred Nobel—quite naturally, as in those times mathematics did not directly affect the lives of people. Moreover, Nobel was a technologist rather than a pure science man.

Nobel's final will of 1895 bequeathed 9,000,000 dollars for a foundation whose income would support five annual prizes in physics, chemistry, medicine–physiology, literature, and peace. Four of the original five prizes were in fields which were close to Nobel's own interests, medicine being the exception.

A sixth Nobel Prize in economic science was added in 1969. The addition of this new Nobel Prize suggests the possibility of an addition of a seventh Nobel Prize at some future date. There is a strong case that this new Nobel Prize would be in the mathematical sciences, which could include statistics, computer science, etc. The Nobel equivalent for mathematics is the Fields Medals that are awarded at each International Congress of Mathematicians. But these are given only once in every four years to a mathematician under forty, and not as famous as the other awards.

8

Mysterious Infinity

There was a young fellow from Trinity
who took the square root of infinity
but the number of digits
gave him the fidgets;
He dropped Math and took up Divinity.

George Gamow

The symbol for infinity

$$\infty$$

THE above symbol for infinity was first found in print in Wallis' *Arithmetica Infinitorum* published in 1656. John Wallis (1616–1703), one of the most original English mathematicians of his day, was actually educated at Cambridge to be a doctor for the Church. He entered Holy Orders, but his passion revolved chiefly around the study of mathematics. The *Arithmetica Infinitorum* was his greatest work.

Wallis in his choice for a symbol for infinity might have been influenced by the fact that the Romans commonly used this symbol for a thousand—mainly to denote a large sum, just like we use the word 'myriad' nowadays to denote a large number. The Greeks used the same symbol to denote ten thousand. By the late seventeenth century, the symbol was in common usage.

Although we have first taken up a discussion on the symbol for infinity, the concept of infinity itself has given mathematicians and thinkers problems since the time of the ancient Greeks. For example Zeno (ca BCE 490–430) of Elea in southern Italy, famous for his paradoxes, wondered if magnitudes (lengths or numbers) were infinitely divisible or made up of a large number of small indivisible parts.

A very boring way to start with the mysterious term 'infinity' is to call it 'without limit'. Then the first thing the non-curious and non-adventurous mind would say is, 'If there is no limit, then let's study within limits. As it is, whatever is in the syllabus is *infinitely* tough and dull'.

There is no record of earlier civilisations conceptualising or discussing infinity, although there are some references to infinity in the *Yajurveda*. We can say that the story of infinity definitely begin with the ancient Greeks. Originally the word '*apeiron*' was used to define the concept of what we now know as infinity. It meant unbounded, indefinite, or undefined. It was a negative, even pejorative word. For the Greeks, the original chaos out of which the world was formed was *apeiron*. Aristotle thought being infinite was an adversity not a perfection.

The concept of infinity was forced upon the Greeks from three traditional observations that they obtained from the physical world:

- Time seems without end.
- Space and time can be unendingly sub-divided.
- Space is not bounded.

Aristotle said that the infinite was imperfect, unfinished and unthinkable. Although we nowadays, do not judge infinity so harshly, we still agree that infinity is a puzzling notion. If we needed an example for this statement, we would only have to look at infinite series. An interesting observation with infinite series is that they are not very well behaved.

Let us *feel* the following series:

$$1 - 1 + 1 - 1 + 1 - 1 + \dots$$

If the terms are grouped as below,

$$(1 - 1) + (1 - 1) + (1 - 1) + \dots,$$

then the sum appears to be

$$0 + 0 + 0 + \dots\dots = 0.$$

But if the terms are grouped differently,

$$1 + (-1 + 1) + (-1 + 1) + (-1 + 1) + \dots,$$

then the sum appears to be

$$1 + 0 + 0 + 0 + \dots = 1.$$

So $0 = 1$. It would of course be incorrect to conclude that $0 = 1$.

Instead, we have to conclude that infinite series do not always obey the traditional rules of algebra, especially those that permit the arbitrary regrouping of terms.

Let us look at another series

$$1 + \frac{1}{2} + \frac{1}{4} + \frac{1}{8} + \frac{1}{16} + \dots\dots$$

Here the sum is always less than 2 but keeps increasing as more terms are added. With each new term, the sum approaches closer and closer to 2 but never quite reaches it. On the other hand, consider the series

$$1 + \frac{1}{2} + \frac{1}{3} + \frac{1}{4} + \frac{1}{5} + \dots\dots$$

The sum becoming larger and larger than any chosen value if sufficient terms are taken, it has no limit. Such a series is called a divergent series.

The *paradox* is the fact that there are just as many even natural numbers in the first series $(1 + 1/2 + 1/4 + 1/8 + 1/16 + \ldots\ldots)$ as there are even and odd numbers altogether in the second series, thus contradicting the notion that *the whole is greater than any of its parts.* This seeming contradiction arises from the properties of collections containing an infinite number of objects. Since both are infinite, they are for both practical and mathematical purposes equal.

Consider the following *sequence* or list of numbers:

$$1, \frac{1}{2}, \frac{1}{3}, \frac{1}{4}, \ldots\ldots, \frac{1}{n}, \ldots$$

This is a sequence whose nth term is $1/n$. Now we can say that the sequence has the limit 0 as n goes to infinity,

$$\frac{1}{n} \to 0 \text{ as } n \to \infty$$

It connotes that as we go further and further into the series, the terms get closer and closer to zero, though never reaching zero. From this, we get the notion of an *infinite series*.

Consider the *partial sums*

$$1$$

$$1\frac{1}{2} = 1 + \frac{1}{2}$$

$$1\frac{3}{4} = 1 + \frac{1}{2} + \frac{1}{4}$$

$$1\frac{7}{8} = 1 + \frac{1}{2} + \frac{1}{4} + \frac{1}{8}$$

$$\ldots\ldots$$

$$1\frac{2047}{2048} = 1 + \frac{1}{2} + \frac{1}{4} + \ldots + \frac{1}{2048}$$

and so on. Now these sums are headed somewhere, namely, towards 2. If you add on enough terms, eventually you will get as close as you like to 2. So we can say that the sum of all the terms is 2, that is

$$\sum_{n=0}^{\infty} \frac{1}{2^n} = 1 + \frac{1}{2} + \frac{1}{4} + \frac{1}{8} + \ldots = 2$$

This is an infinite series that *converges*.

Some series do not converge, like $1 + 1/2 + 1/3 + 1/4 + \ldots$, the series we discussed before. This series is called a *harmonic series*. To see that the partial sums go off to infinity, note that we have 1 and 1/2 and then

$$\frac{1}{3} + \frac{1}{4} > \frac{1}{4} + \frac{1}{4} = \frac{1}{2}$$

$$\frac{1}{5} + \frac{1}{6} + \frac{1}{7} + \frac{1}{8} > \frac{1}{8} + \frac{1}{8} + \frac{1}{8} + \frac{1}{8} = \frac{1}{2},$$

the next 8 terms,

$$\frac{1}{9} + \frac{1}{10} + \ldots + \frac{1}{16} > 8 \times \frac{1}{16} = \frac{1}{2}$$

and so on. So our sum grows larger than any multiple of 1/2. We say that the harmonic series *diverges*. Now a question may arise in the reader's mind—'Can infinity be halved?' This and more questions have puzzled humanity since ancient times. They argued that it must have an end. Was it the limitation of the human mind or a question GOD never wanted to answer nor let us know about?

Many issues about infinity have been resolved through the ages, but a clear definition of it still remains elusive.

Rules for infinity

Infinity also has a set of rules for arithmetical operations.

With itself

$$\infty + \infty = \infty$$

$$\infty \times \infty = \infty$$

$$-\infty + (-\infty) = -\infty$$

$$-\infty \times (-\infty) = \infty$$

$$\infty \times (-\infty) = -\infty$$

Undefined operations

There are certain undefined operations:

$$0 \times \infty$$

$$\infty + (-\infty)$$

$$\frac{\infty}{\infty}$$

It is important to realise that $x/\infty = 0$ is not equivalent to $0 \times \infty = x$. If this were true, then it would have to be true for every x, which would mean that all numbers are equal, an impossible proposition. Thus $0 \times \infty$ remains undefined, or *indeterminate*.

Last word: Hotel Infinity

The great mathematician David Hilbert (1873–1943) was often asked to explain the curious nature of infinity. To shed light upon the mystery, he developed a novel thought experiment:

Imagine a hypothetical hotel with an infinite number of rooms. One day a new guest arrives and is disappointed to hear that, despite the hotel's infinite size, it has no vacancies. Fortunately the clerk (Hilbert) has a solution. He simply asks each of the guests to move to the next room: the guest in room 1 moves to room 2, the guest in room 2 to room 3, and so on. This allows the new arrival to slip into the newly vacant room (1). So far so good . . .

The following night, however, Hilbert is presented with a more challenging problem—the arrival of an infinitely large number of new guests. Hilbert, delighted by the prospect of infinitely more hotel bills, once again has a solution. He simply asks each guest to move to the room whose number is twice that of his or her current room: the guest in room 1 moves to room 2, the guest in room 2 moves to room 4, and so on. Everyone still has a room but an infinite number of rooms have been vacated for the new arrivals!

9

Misunderstood Calculus

The word 'calculus' stems from the nascent development of mathematics: the early Greeks used pebbles arranged in patterns to learn arithmetic and geometry. The Latin word for 'pebble' is 'calculus', a diminutive of *calx* (genitive *calcis*) meaning 'limestone'.

Calculus is probably the most important development in mathematics. It is applied in physics for the study of all natural systems, mathematical modelling and as a general method whenever the goal is an optimum solution to a problem that can be given a mathematical form.

Calculus is built on two major complementary ideas. The first is *differential calculus*, which studies the rate of change in one quantity relative to the rate of change in another quantity. This can be illustrated by the slope of a line. The second is *integral calculus*, which studies the accumulation of quantities, such as areas under a curve, linear distance travelled, or volume displaced.

The simplest definition that can be offered is that calculus is the study of mathematically defined change. Examples of typical differential calculus problems include:

- finding the acceleration and speed of a free-falling body at a particular moment.
- finding the optimal number of units a company should produce to maximise their profit.

Examples of integral calculus problems include:

- finding the amount of water pumped by a motor with a fixed power input but varying conditions of pumping losses and pressure.
- finding the amount of grass mowed by a lawn mower of given power with varying density of grass.

Newton (1643–1727) invented calculus to determine the speed of an object moving in one dimension. Speed is simply the distance travelled by the time taken. But in advanced science, with gravity as the force causing the motion, the function becomes continuous and not discrete. Thus the velocity of the object is derivative of x, the distance with respect to time t.

$$\nu = \frac{dx}{dt}, \text{ which is actually } \lim_{\Delta t \to 0} \frac{\Delta x}{\Delta t},$$

here Δx and Δt are infinitesimal distance and time respectively.

Suppose you were asked to find out the rate at which the universe is expanding with the following information in hand:

Let t be the time that has elapsed since the Big Bang. In that time, light, travelling at speed c, would have been able to travel a maximum distance, ct. The portion of the universe that we can observe is therefore a sphere of radius ct, with volume,

$$v = \frac{4}{3}\pi r^3 = \frac{4}{3}\pi (ct)^3.$$

Differential calculus will tell us to differentiate velocity, which is

$$\frac{dv}{dt} = \frac{4}{3}\pi c^3.3t^2.$$

Without going into the details of the rules for differentiation, we find that rate of expansion is proportional to $c^3.t^2$—which is huge; you can well imagine the enormous rate at which we are expanding! Next let us see what integral calculus has to do with our lives.

Work is a measure of the amount of energy transferred by a force. If a locomotive sets a wagon in motion, the locomotive's force on the wagon transfers energy to the wagon. If F is the force applied on the wagon and it moves by a distance x, then to find out the work done, we can multiply the force F, several times in very small intervals of time. These very small values are called infinitesimal.

Here we use the integration of this infinitesimal work done to find out the total work done.

If dW is infinitesimal work done and dx is the infinitesimal distance, then we have

$$dW = F.dx$$

If the wagon moved from position a to b then total work done, W is

$$W = \int_a^b F.dx$$

This is integral calculus.

The very word *calculus* seems to send shivers to the backbones of students and blanks their minds which suddenly fills with huge *Greeky*, cryptic equations. But, in fact, it is the easiest of all branches of mathematics. It is straightforward and can be visualised easily. Next time, try to remove the mental block and understand that there is nothing to be scared of.

The restricted meaning of *calculus,* meaning differential and integral calculus, is due to Leibniz. Newton did not originally use the term, he preferred *method of fluxions*. He used the term *calculus differentialis* in a memorandum written in 1691.

Newton and Leibniz independently developed calculus—although Leibniz started with integration while Newton with differentiation. But the credit for propagation of calculus goes to Newton.

10

Four Fours

By now the reader might have got slightly bored with the huge injections of 'knowledge' that they have been subjected to till now. But now, I will regale you with some interesting facts. I have been told (and I have checked—it is true!) that there is a way by which we can write all the numbers from 1 to 100 using just four fours and any mathematical expression.

Here are a few examples; the rest are for you to discover.

1	$\frac{4+4-4}{4}$
2	$\frac{4 \times 4}{4+4}$
4	$(4-4) \times 4 + 4$
14	$4 + 4 + 4 + \sqrt{4}$
25	$4! + \sqrt{4} - \frac{4}{4}$
50	$44 + \frac{4!}{4}$
82	$4 \times (4! - 4) + \sqrt{4}$
100	$4 \times 4! + \sqrt{4} + \sqrt{4}$

You can use all arithmetical operators. Special operators like factorial, square root and power operators are also allowed. Interestingly, there is more than one way to express the numbers.

11

Happy Numbers

Most human endeavour is motivated by the search for happiness; some people are intrinsically happy and do not have to search for happiness outside themselves. Even some numbers are intrinsically happy.

A number is called happy if the sum of the squares of its digits, and then the sum of the squares of the digits of this sum and so on, ends in 1.

For example

$$4599 \Rightarrow 4^2 + 5^2 + 9^2 + 9^2 = 203$$

$$203 \Rightarrow 2^2 + 0^2 + 3^2 = 13$$

$$13 \Rightarrow 1^2 + 3^2 = 10$$

$$10 \Rightarrow 1^2 + 0^2 = 1$$

Can you try and find out some more happy numbers?

Any number formed with digits 9, 8, 5, 2, 1 and 1 such as 129851 will be happy as

$$9^2 + 8^2 + 5^2 + 2^2 + 1^2 + 1^2 = 176$$

and 176 itself is a happy number.

It is tempting to search for more such numbers, as this endeavour leads to some very interesting properties of numbers.

12

The Five Nines

Consider the following expressions:

$$9+\frac{99}{99}$$

$$9+9-9+\frac{9}{9}$$

$$\left\{9+\frac{9}{9}\right\}\times\frac{9}{9}$$

$$9+\frac{9+9}{9+9}$$

$$9+\frac{9\times 9}{9\times 9}$$

$$\sqrt{9}+\sqrt{9}+\sqrt{9}+\frac{9}{9}$$

$$9^{\frac{9}{9}}+\frac{9}{9}$$

Does your mathematical sense trigger? All these result in ten. *Five nines to make a ten*! Find some more expressions like these. Believe me, there are at least four more ways.

13

The Good Number 24

The number 24 is very interesting. It can be obtained by using the same digits three times with any mathematical symbol. For example,

$$8 + 8 + 8 = 24$$

Try it with other numbers:

$$22 + 2 = 24$$

$$3^3 - 3 = 24$$

$$4! \times (4/4) = 24$$

$$5!/\sqrt{5 \times 5} = 24$$

$$(\sqrt{9})! + 9 + 9 = 24$$

$$(\sqrt{9})^{(\sqrt{9})} - (\sqrt{9}) = 24$$

There are more such expressions. Trying to find them will be well worth the effort.

14

Sum Equal to Product, Really

There are some pairs of numbers which exhibit an interesting property—the product of the numbers is equal to their sum.

For example,

$$3 \text{ and } 1.5 \qquad 3 \times 1.5 = 4.5 \qquad 3 + 1.5 = 4.5$$

$$3.5 \text{ and } 1.4 \qquad 3.5 \times 1.4 = 4.9 \qquad 3.5 + 1.4 = 4.9$$

In general if $a = \frac{b}{b-1}$, then $a + b = ab$.

Well, does there exist a triad of three numbers whose sum is equal to their product?

Let us see.

Consider the triad: 7.5, 1.66 and 0.8. The sum of these three numbers is 9.96; their product also is 9.96.

Try finding out some more numbers (without reading the next line).

In general, $abc = a + b + c$ if $c = \frac{a+b}{ab-1}$.

Let us now have a look at the famous 7–11 store problem.

Once in the 'seven–eleven' (7–11) store, a customer selected four items to buy. The cashier at the counter, instead of adding the costs of the items, multiplied them and obtained *exactly* 7.11, the very name of the store! The customer angered at the cashier's stupidity, tells him to add and not multiply the costs. You can imagine his astonishment when he found that the total was still Rs 7.11!

What do you think was the exact costs of the four items?

SOLUTION $3.16 + 1.25 + 1.50 + 1.20$

There are a few more numbers like these. Look at the following:

$$6.44 = 1.84 + 1.75 + 1.60 + 1.25$$

$$6.51 = 2.00 + 1.86 + 1.40 + 1.25$$

Keep trying and you will find lots of such numbers. 'Mathematicate' and meditate!

15

Multiplication Table

I proceeded for the most frightful experience of my life.

Multiplication table of seven

You must be wondering, 'why seven—of all the tables to be frightened of, why seven?' Well, I found it difficult because it has apparently no pattern—being mid-way between 5 and 10. But conforming to the system, I crammed up the tables of 1, 2, 3, 4, 5, 6, 7, 8, 9 and 10. I still wonder if there is a need for this exercise, as in real life, there is hardly a calculation done using these tables—what with the advent of calculators in watches, address diaries and cell phones. The pedagogue's justification for this most boring arithmetical task is,

'*The multiplication tables are a terrific tool for building the skill of memorization essential to learning during the grammar stage of the educational process.*'

But there are rewards in completing the arduous task of memorising the tables. We can discover some interesting patterns in them.

For example, consider the multiplication tables of 9. Look at the first digits of the table—they increase from 0 to 9.

The second digit decreases from 9 to 0. So in fact, there is no need to memorise this table. We just need to write the numbers as:

0	1	2	3	4	5	6	7	8	9
9	8	7	6	5	4	3	2	1	0

There we have the table of nine!

There is even an easy way out of memorising the table of 7. I used the famous deductive technology of mathematical learning. Add to each number in the table of 5 (5, 10, 15, 20, 25, 30, 35, 40, 45, 50) in increasing order starting from top, the number in the table of 2 (2, 4, 6, 8, 10, 12, 14, 16, 18, 20) and we get the table of 7!

Here is a short cut to multiplying nine by seven. Count the seventh finger from the right and bend it:

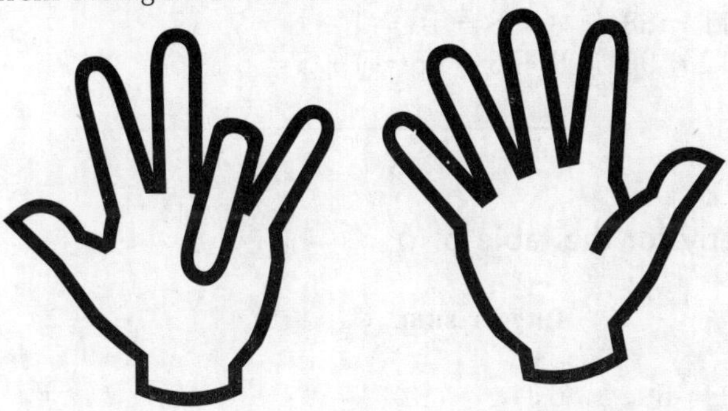

There are six fingers to the right of the bent finger, and three fingers to the left. So we have $9 \times 7 = 63$. It works!

Some simple facts

- To multiply a number by five, multiply a half of that number by ten.
- When you need to multiply a number by two, just add the number to itself.
- To multiply numbers that differ by two, multiply the number between them by itself and subtract one.

Interesting property of the table of 8

	Integer sum		
$8 \times 1 = 8$	8	8	
$8 \times 2 = 16$	$1 + 6 = 7$	7	Do you see
$8 \times 3 = 24$	$2 + 4 = 6$	6	the pattern?
$8 \times 4 = 32$	$3 + 2 = 5$	5	Sequence
$8 \times 5 = 40$	$4 + 0 = 4$	4	9 to 1 repeats.
$8 \times 6 = 48$	$4 + 8 = 12 = 1 + 2 = 3$	3	
$8 \times 7 = 56$	$5 + 6 = 11 = 1 + 1 = 2$	2	
$8 \times 8 = 64$	$6 + 4 = 10 = 1 + 0 = 1$	1	I wish I had
$8 \times 9 = 72$	$7 + 2 = 9$	9	known this
$8 \times 10 = 80$	$8 + 0 = 8$	8	before!
$8 \times 11 = 88$	$8 + 8 = 16 = 1 + 6 = 7$	7	
$8 \times 12 = 96$	$9 + 6 = 15 = 1 + 5 = 6$	6	

Similarly for the table of 6

	Integer sum		
$6 \times 1 = 6$	6	6	
$6 \times 2 = 12$	$1+2 = 3$	3	
$6 \times 3 = 18$	$1+8 = 9$	9	Do you see
$6 \times 4 = 24$	$2+4 = 6$	6	the pattern?
$6 \times 5 = 30$	$3+0 = 3$	3	6, 3, 9 repeats.
$6 \times 6 = 36$	$3+6 = 9$	9	
$6 \times 7 = 42$	$4+2 = 6$	6	It is an easy
$6 \times 8 = 48$	$4+8 = 12 = 1+2 = 3$	3	way to
$6 \times 9 = 54$	$5+4 = 9$	9	remember.
$6 \times 10 = 60$	$6+0 = 6$	6	
$6 \times 11 = 66$	$6+6 = 12 = 1+2 = 3$	3	
$6 \times 12 = 72$	$7+2 = 9$	9	

16

Divisibility Funda

A very important aspect of arithmetic in school is the rule for divisibility. There are standard rules for determining whether a number is divisible by 2, 3, 4, 5, 6, 8, 9, 11 etc. But for numbers like 7, 13 and so on, there are no rules found in textbooks. But there is no cause for worry—some great mathematician has simplified things and there is now a rule for almost all numbers. We shall explore them in this chapter.

In school we are taught a few basic rules which are summarised thus: A number is

Divisible by	If
2	the last digit is divisible by two
3	the sum of the digits of the number is divisible by three
4	the last two digits are divisible by four
5	the last digit is 5 or 0
6	the number is divisible by 2 and by 3
8	the last three digits are divisible by 8
9	the sum of the digits of the number is divisible by nine
10	the last digit is 0

You will notice that there is one number missing here—the rule for seven. Your teacher might have informed you that seven does not have any definite rule for divisibility. This got me thinking. I kept wondering and pondering till I found a rule-of-thumb law for divisibility by 7. It is a bit different but I think quite apt.

The rule for 7: The $L - 2M$ rule

The last digit of the number is doubled and subtracted from the remaining number. The procedure is repeated till a number is obtained which can be identified easily as being divisible by 7 or not.

Suppose the number is 6125.

STEP 1 $612 - (5 \times 2) = 612 - 10 = 602$
Here 5, the last digit is doubled and subtracted from the remaining number. We now use the result, 602 for the iterative process. The last digit, 2 is doubled and subtracted from 60.

STEP 2 $60 - (2 \times 2) = 60 - 4 = 56$ which is 7×8, hence 6125 is divisible by 7.

Try a few numbers, and then you will really appreciate the technique.

The same rule can be extrapolated to apply for 13, 17 and 19.

For 13 $L + 4M$

For 17 $L - 5M$

For 19 $L + 2M$

where M denotes the last digit and L, the remaining number.

Suppose we were to test the divisibility of 9994 with 19. Using the $L + 2M$ rule which means that the last digit is doubled and *added* to the remaining number,

STEP 1 $999 + 8 = 1007$

STEP 2 $100 + 14 = 114$

STEP 3 $11 + 8 = 19$ itself, so 9994 is divisible by 19.

In Vedic mathematics, there is a divisibility rule or algorithm for almost any number. It involves finding the *Ekādhika* (a special multiplier) of the divisor and a method of osculation—an iterative process of multiplication and addition/subtraction operations which reduces the number to a smaller number which is easily observable as divisible or not. We shall not go into the details for calculating the *Ekādhika* of the divisor, but will explain the procedure for checking divisibility.

Let us understand what 'osculation' actually means. Suppose you were to 'osculate' 21 with 5, to find if 21 was divisible by 7; we could multiply the last digit with 5 i.e. $5 \times 1 = 5$, add this to the previous digit 2 and thus get 7. This is the simplest of osculations as it involves only two operations. A few more illustrative examples will come in handy.

4321 with 7

$432 + 1 \times 7 = 439$

$43 + 9 \times 7 = 106$

$10 + 6 \times 7 = 52$

$5 + 2 \times 7 = 19$

$1 + 9 \times 7 = 64$

and so on to get 34, 31, 10 and finally 1.

The purpose of osculation, as mentioned before, is to reach a number which is easily identifiable as divisible, or not.

Let us now examine the *Ekādhika* (without actually going into the calculation behind it) for some numbers:

1. For 9, 19, 29, 39, . . . they are 1, 2, 3, 4, . . . respectively
2. For 3, 13, 23, 33, . . . they are 1, 4, 7, 10, . . . respectively
3. For 7, 17, 27, 37, . . . they are 5, 12, 19, 26 . . . respectively
4. For 1, 11, 21, 31, . . . they are 1, 10, 19, 28 . . . respectively

Osculation by the *Ekādhika*

Let us again check the divisibility of 9994 by 19.

(i)	The *Ekādhika* for 19 is 2, so multiply the last digit by 2 and add the product 8 to the previous digit 9.	9994 $4 \times 2 = 8$ $8 + 9 = 17$ 99 left
(ii)	Now osculate 17 with 2 to get 15 $(7\times2+1)$; add 15 to the last digit of the remaining number i.e. 9 to get 24.	17 $1 + 7 \times 2 = 15$ $15 + 9 = 24$ 9 left
(iii)	Now osculate 24 with 2 to get 10 $(4\times2+2)$; add 10 to the remaining digit 9 to get 19 which is a multiple of 19; hence 9994 is divisible by 19.	24 $2 + 4 \times 2 = 10$ $10 + 9 = 19$

This is one way. The other way is to simply osculate with the *Ekādhika*. The method has to be chosen keeping in mind the ease of calculation; sometimes the above method is simpler.

Do you realise how simple it is? The only thing to remember is the osculator or the *Ekādhika*, which we can do so with a few mnemonics. Perhaps this is the greatest contribution of Vedic mathematics.

Let us find out whether 7755 is divisible by 33 using the straight osculation method.

The *Ekādhika* for 33 is 10. Thus for 7755

$$775 + 50 = 825 \Rightarrow 82 + 50 = 132 \Rightarrow 13 + 20 = 33$$

This is a simply terrific process! Something all middle school students must explore. But there is a slight problem. For numbers ending with 1 and 7, the process may become cumbersome, as the *Ekādhika* is a higher order number like 5, 12, 19, 26 etc. For these numbers another brilliant solution is the negative osculation method. Here the principle is the same except that the operation used is subtraction instead of addition and if the end result is a multiple of the number or zero (*which is true for most cases*), the divisibility is proved.

If P is the positive osculator and N, the negative one, then the rule is divisor,

$$D = P + N.$$

For number 7, $P = 5$, thus $N = 7 - 5 = 2$.

For number 21, $P = 19$, thus $N = 21 - 19 = 2$.

The negative osculators for some numbers are:

For 7, 17, 27, 37, . . . they are 2, 5, 8, 11 . . . . . . respectively.

For 11, 21, 31, 41, . . . they are 1, 2, 3, 4 . . . . . . respectively.

To obtain the osculator, all we have to keep in mind is that we have to multiply the number to get a product ending in 1. Remove the 1 and the remaining number is the negative osculator.

The important thing to remember is that unlike the positive osculation, here we have to osculate by *subtracting* the product of the *Ekādhika and the last digit.*

Let us consider an example to make things clear:

We will test the divisibility of 165763 with 41. The negative osculator is 4.

$$16576 - 4 \times 3 = 16564$$

$$1656 - 4 \times 4 = 1640$$

$$164 - 4 \times 0 = 164$$

$$16 - 4 \times 4 = 0$$

Let us consider another example: Whether 10171203 is divisible by 67. Here we will multiply 67 by 3 which is 201; hence the negative osculator is 20.

$$1017120 - 20 \times 3 = 1017060$$

$$101706 - 20 \times 0 = 101706$$

$$10170 - 20 \times 6 = 10050$$

$$1005 - 20 \times 0 = 1005$$

$$100 - 20 \times 5 = 0$$

Thus it is divisible

Here you see how easy division has become with simple arithmetic. Happy dividing!

17

Printer's Errors

I discovered a very interesting book on mathematical recreations, H. E. Dudeney's *Amusements in Mathematics*. All his recreations impressed me but I found this particular one called 'printer's error' truly remarkable.

A printer when required to set the type for the number $2^5 \cdot 9^2$, *mistakenly set it as 2592 (the dot was meant to indicate multiplication). However, upon proofreading, the number was still found to be written correctly.*

Because $2^5 \cdot 9^2 = 2592$

During the course of reading the book, a few more errors were discovered.

$$1129\frac{1}{3} = 11^2 \cdot \left(9\frac{1}{3}\right)$$

$$2124\frac{9}{11} = 21^2 \cdot \left(4\frac{9}{11}\right)$$

$$34425 = 3^4 \cdot 425$$

$$312325 = 31^2 \cdot 325$$

Try finding some more like these—it is a meditative experience. Some interesting *dottable fractions* which are a kind of printer's error are given:

$$\frac{416}{21879} = \frac{4 \cdot 16}{2 \cdot 187 \cdot 9}$$

$$\frac{666}{64676} = \frac{6 \cdot 6 \cdot 6}{6 \cdot 46 \cdot 76}$$

$$\frac{388}{485} = \frac{3 \cdot 8 \cdot 8}{48 \cdot 5}$$

These are just a few *dottable fractions*—there are several such fractions. It would be interesting to find out where to place the dots in the following fractions to make them dottable.

$$\frac{12980}{74635} \qquad \frac{34560}{91728}$$

$$\frac{13680}{29754} \qquad \frac{46350}{12978}$$

$$\frac{13950}{46872} \qquad \frac{54270}{18693}$$

$$\frac{17460}{39285} \qquad \frac{78360}{21549}$$

$$\frac{18630}{27945} \qquad \frac{86310}{92475}$$

$$\frac{32160}{97485} \qquad \frac{92460}{37185}$$

Using the number of the beast:[1]

$$\frac{666}{998} \qquad \frac{666}{4995}$$

$$\frac{666}{3478} \qquad \frac{666}{27972}$$

$$\frac{666}{38665}$$

[1] The number of the beast (666) is a concept from the Bible. It is said that the number 666 identifies the Antichrist, the embodiment of all evil.

18

Digital Variants

This chapter is dedicated to some amusing types of numbers that are really interesting to explore and observe. I do not even remember where they originated from—I used to pen them down in my diary as and when I found them, not being too particular about writing down their sources.

Observe the numbers given below:

$$12\,33 = 12^2 + 33^2$$

$$990\,100 = 990^2 + 100^2$$

$$9412\,2353 = 9412^2 + 2353^2$$

$$74160\,43776 = 74160^2 + 43776^2$$

$$116788\,321168 = 116788^2 + 321168^2$$

The sum of the squares of the two halves of the number is equal to the number itself.

I later found that there exist numbers which are equal to the difference of the squares of their halves, e.g. $48 = 8^2 - 4^2$.

Can you find some more numbers like this? A few more are:

$34\,68 = 68^2 - 34^2$

$$3334\,6668 = 6668^2 - 3334^2$$

If you were a number maniac, you would not stop there. Your obsession would make you wonder if there are numbers which split three-ways and the cube of the parts equal the whole:

$$22\,18\,59 = 22^3 + 18^3 + 59^3$$

$$166\,500\,333 = 166^3 + 500^3 + 333^3$$

And this one is even more complex:

$$336 = (3^1 + 3^1 + 6^1) + (3^2 + 3^2 + 6^2) + (3^3 + 3^3 + 6^3)$$

A factorial is expressed mathematically as below:

$$n! = 1 \times 2 \times 3 \times 4 \ldots\ldots (n-1) \times n$$

It does not seem possible that a number can be equal to the sum of the factorial of its digits, does it? But look below.

$$145 = 1! + 4! + 5!$$

$$40585 = 4! + 0! + 5! + 8! + 5!$$

Also,

$$4! + 1 = 52 \qquad 5! + 1 = 112 \qquad 7! + 1 = 712$$

These are called Brown's numbers, and there can be more of these which will be fascinating to find.

Look at the expressions below:

$$4150 = 4^5 + 1^5 + 5^5 + 0^5$$

$$4151 = 4^5 + 1^5 + 5^5 + 1^5$$

$$194979 = 1^5 + 9^5 + 4^5 + 9^5 + 7^5 + 9^5$$

These are called *perfect digital invariants*. A PDI is a number equal to the sum of a power of its digits when the *power is not equal to the length of the number.*

An interesting pattern called the *pluperfect digital invariants* or PPDIs is found next. They are also called *Armstrong numbers*. In each case, the power corresponds to the number of digits.

$$153 = 1^3 + 5^3 + 3^3$$

$$1634 = 1^4 + 6^4 + 3^4 + 4^4$$

$$54748 = 5^5 + 4^5 + 7^5 + 4^5 + 8^5$$

$$548834 = 5^6 + 4^6 + 8^6 + 8^6 + 3^6 + 4^6$$

$$1741725 = 1^7 + 7^7 + 4^7 + 1^7 + 7^7 + 2^7 + 5^7$$

The following numbers are unique in the sense that they use their digits to reproduce themselves through mathematical operators—a very intriguing experience even to contemplate. These numbers are called *repdigit Friedman's number*.

$$11111111111 = \frac{(11-1)^{11} - 1 \times 1}{11 - 1 - 1}$$

$$2222222222222 = \frac{2\left(\dfrac{22-2}{2}\right)^{2\wedge(2+2)-2} - 2}{\left(2 + \dfrac{2}{2}\right)^2}$$

(the symbol '∧' means to the power of)

$$333333333 = \frac{\left(3 \times 3 + \dfrac{3}{3}\right)^{3 \times 3} - \left(\dfrac{3}{3}\right)}{3}$$

$$444444444444444 = \frac{4\left(\dfrac{44}{4} - \dfrac{4}{4}\right)^{4 \times 4 - \frac{4}{4}} - 4}{4 + 4 + \left(\dfrac{4}{4}\right)}$$

$$5555555555 = \frac{5(5+5)^{5+5} - 5}{5 + 5 - \left(\dfrac{5}{5}\right)}$$

$$6666666666666666 = \frac{6\left(\frac{66-6}{6}\right)^{6+\frac{66-6}{6}} - 6}{6 + \frac{6+6+6}{6}}$$

$$77777777777777 = \frac{7\left(\frac{777}{7}\right)^{7+7} - 7 + 7 - 7}{7 + \frac{7+7}{7}}$$

$$88888888888888 = \frac{8\left(\frac{888}{8}\right)^{8+8-\left(\frac{8+8}{8}\right)} - 8}{8 + \left(\frac{8}{8}\right)}$$

$$99999999 = \left(9 + \frac{9}{9}\right)^{9-\frac{9}{9}} - \frac{9}{9}$$

A *Friedman number* is a positive integer which can be written in some non-trivial way using its own digits, together with the symbols $+, -, \times, /, ^\wedge, ()$ and concatenation. They can be perfect or normal. The difference will be evident from the following examples:

$64550 = (6^4 - 5) \times 50$ Perfect

$16875 = 1 \times 68 + 7^5$ Perfect

$25872 = 528 \times 7^2$ Normal

$37875 = 75 \times (8^3 - 7)$ Normal

In the first two cases above, the digits are used in the order of the number's formation, hence they are called perfect. Friedman's numbers are surprisingly common—there are about 75 such numbers below 9999. A few of them are:

25, 1206, 2187, 2500, 3125, 4096, 4628, 9261

Can you find out how? Believe me, it's an interesting exercise.

Try the Friedman's number using all nine digits,

$$123456789 = \frac{(86 + 2 \times 7)^5 - 91}{3^4}$$

$$987654321 = \frac{8 \times \left(97 + \frac{6}{2}\right)^5 + 1}{3^4}$$

Some more interesting numbers are:

$$8833 = 88^2 + 33^2$$

$$9474 = 9^4 + 4^4 + 7^4 + 4^4$$

$$594 = 1^5 + 2^9 + 3^4$$

$$732 = 1^7 + 2^6 + 3^5 + 4^4 + 5^3 + 6^2 + 7^1$$

Observe the powers and base.

$$1033 = 8^1 + 8^0 + 8^3 + 8^3$$

$$3413 = 1^1 + 2^2 + 3^3 + 4^4 + 5^5$$

$$3435 = 3^3 + 4^4 + 3^3 + 5^5$$

The following numbers are called the common base numbers. Notice that the base is common and that the powers coincide with the digits of the number.

$$4624 = 4^4 + 4^6 + 4^2 + 4^4$$

$$1033 = 8^1 + 8^0 + 8^3 + 8^3$$

$$595968 = 4^5 + 4^9 + 4^5 + 4^9 + 4^6 + 4^8$$

$$3909511 = 5^3 + 5^9 + 5^0 + 5^9 + 5^5 + 5^1 + 5^1$$

$$13177388 = 7^1 + 7^3 + 7^1 + 7^7 + 7^7 + 7^3 + 7^8 + 7^8$$

$$52135640 = 19^5 + 19^2 + 19^1 + 19^3 + 19^5 + 19^6 + 19^4 + 19^0$$

The beauty of numbers lie here—some seemingly obscure number can be represented in truly amazing ways. Above are a few ways of looking at numbers. Searching for Friedman's numbers is a truly intriguing experience as each number can be calculated in several different ways. These numbers can also be found for base systems other than the decimal system.

I will bring to your notice just one more pair of interesting numbers and then leave you to ponder on the wonder of it all.

$$203313 \times 657624 = 426756 \times 313302$$

The right side is the reverse of the left side!

In a lighter vein, a joke to relieve your mind after the number of mathematical operations you may have carried out in this chapter:

Dean, to the physics department, 'Why do I always have to give you guys so much money for laboratories and expensive equipment and stuff.

Why couldn't you be like the mathematics department—all they need is money for pencils, paper and waste-paper baskets.

Or even better, like the philosophy department. All they need are pencils and paper.'

19

0123456789 and More

In the previous chapters, I have showed you the wonder of numbers. But what fascinates me the most is the use of all the numbers—0 to 9. There are so many wondrous things which can be done using *all* the numbers!

Using all the numbers, I could find two ways of getting 100 by placing any mathematical operator i.e. +, −, ×, / and () between the numbers.

$$1 + 2 + 3 + 4 + 5 + 6 + 7 + 8 \times 9 = 100$$

$$((1 + 2) \times 3) + (4 \times 5) + 6 + (7 \times 8) + 9 = 100$$

There are at least four more ways to do so. Let's see if you can do it.

PROBLEM 1

Can you find the numbers which can do the following?

$$\begin{array}{r} 1\,2\,3\,4\,5\,6\,7\,8\,9 \\ \times\ \square\square\square\square\square\square\square\square\square\square \\ \hline \square\square\square\square\square\square\square\square\square\square\,9\,8\,7\,6\,5\,4\,3\,2\,1 \end{array}$$

NOTE The set of blanks in the product denotes that 987654321 need only be a part of a bigger number.

PROBLEM 2

Here is a very interesting problem, which I leave to you to solve.

Use the digits 0 to 9 in such a manner, that the resulting number has the following property: Starting from the left, the first digit is divisible by 1, the next two together by 2, the next three by 3 and so on till 10. That is, if the number is *abcdefghij*, then the whole number is divisible by 10; after removing the last digit i.e. j, nine digits are left and the resulting number is divisible by nine, and so forth.

HINT The digit at the 5th place will be 5 and that at the 10th place will be 0.

PROBLEM 3

The next problem is elementary, my dear reader.

Fill in the boxes with the numbers 1, 2, 3, 4, 5, 6, 7, 8, and 9 to make the multiplication equation work.

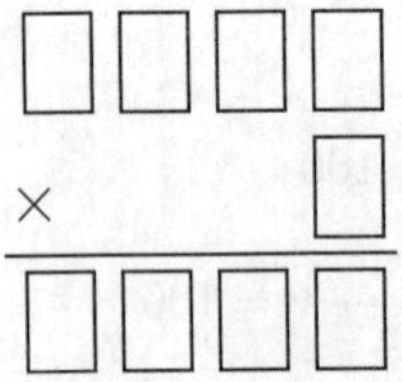

Here is another example of an interesting discovery I made:

$$85555^2 - 1 = 7319658024$$

$$97777^2 - 1 = 9560341728$$

In both these cases, the number when squared is *one more* than a number which contains all the ten digits.

There are certain numbers which are of the form $abc \times de = fg \times hi$, where all the digits from 1 to 9 are used. Here is an example:

$$158 \times 23 = 3634 = 79 \times 46$$

There are at least two more known to me—find out more.

Another 1 to 9 puzzle!!

Using the digits 1 to 9, three numbers (of three digits each) can be formed, such that the second number is twice the first number, and the third number is three times the first number.

HINT There are four solutions. One of them is 192, 384, and 576.

Sum and product

Is there a way in which we can write a sum which uses all the digits (0–9) only once?

876 + 429 = 1305 is one example. How many different ways are there to do this? Think, try it yourself and only then read ahead.

879 + 426 = 1305

859 + 347 = 1206

789 + 264 = 1053

657 + 432 = 1089

756 + 342 = 1098

589 + 473 = 1062

The same question may be asked for products. There are 22 solutions known. A few of them are elucidated below.

$58401 = 63 \times 927$

$19084 = 52 \times 367$

$16038 = 27 \times 594$ or 54×297

$65821 = 7 \times 9403$

$36508 = 4 \times 9127$

$27504 = 3 \times 9168$

$20754 = 3 \times 6918$

Some interesting patterns

The digits 0 to 9 also make some interesting patterns:

$$1 \times 8 + 1 = 9$$
$$12 \times 8 + 2 = 98$$
$$123 \times 8 + 3 = 987$$
$$1234 \times 8 + 4 = 9876$$
$$12345 \times 8 + 5 = 98765$$
$$123456 \times 8 + 6 = 987654$$
$$1234567 \times 8 + 7 = 9876543$$
$$12345678 \times 8 + 8 = 98765432$$
$$123456789 \times 8 + 9 = 987654321$$

$$0 \times 9 + 1 = 1$$
$$1 \times 9 + 2 = 11$$
$$1 \times 9 + 2 = 11$$
$$12 \times 9 + 3 = 111$$
$$123 \times 9 + 4 = 1111$$
$$1234 \times 9 + 5 = 11111$$
$$12345 \times 9 + 6 = 111111$$
$$123456 \times 9 + 7 = 1111111$$
$$1234567 \times 9 + 8 = 11111111$$
$$12345678 \times 9 + 9 = 111111111$$
$$123456789 \times 9 + 10 = 1111111111$$

Special square numbers

The smallest and largest square numbers using all ten digits are given below:

$$1026753849 = 32043^2$$

$$9814072356 = 99066^2$$

Getting hundred

Remember how in the beginning of this chapter, we found ways of getting 100 using any of the mathematical operators. There is a variant to this problem. By only inserting '+' and '–' signs between 1 2 3 4 5 6 7 8 9 (in order), can you get all the numbers between 1 and 100? Below are a few examples:

$$1+2+3+4-5+6+7-8-9=1$$

$$123-4-5-6-7+8-9=100$$

Still another 1 to 9 puzzle

There are at least 30 different square numbers, which use each of the digits (1 to 9) just once. Try finding out some. Besides the fact that it is interesting, you'll learn several properties of numbers.

Two examples are given below:

$$215\,384\,976 = 14\,676^2$$

$$743\,816\,529 = 27\,273^2$$

Look at these sets of numbers

1 9 25 36 784

and

9 25 361 784

Can you find anything special about them? If you examine them carefully, you will notice that they are squares individually and together, the set contains the digits 1 to 9 just once. Find some more such sequences.

Here is another interesting problem: which two numbers (which combined contain all the nine digits) will, when multiplied together, produce another number (the *highest possible*) also containing all the nine digits? Zero is not allowed.

Some examples are given below:

$$8,745,231 \times 96 = 839,542,176$$

$$51,249,876 \times 3 = 153,749,628$$

$$16,583,742 \times 9 = 149,253,678$$

$$32,547,891 \times 6 = 195,287,346$$

100 mixed up with 123456789

Is it possible to write 100 in the form of a mixed number, using all the nine digits once, and only once?

Here is one way of doing it: $91\frac{5742}{638}$.

Actually there are 11 ways to do it including the example. Try finding them yourself before proceeding further.

$96\frac{2148}{537}$	$91\frac{5823}{647}$
$96\frac{1752}{438}$	$82\frac{3546}{197}$
$96\frac{1428}{357}$	$81\frac{7524}{396}$
$94\frac{1578}{263}$	$81\frac{5643}{297}$
$91\frac{7524}{836}$	$3\frac{69258}{714}$

Discussion and solutions

PROBLEM 1: SOLUTION

$$\begin{array}{r} 123456789 \\ \times\ 989010989 \\ \hline 122100120\ 987654321 \end{array}$$

Problem 2: Solution

The number 3816547290 has the required unique property of being divisible by 10, 9, 8, 7, 6, 5, 4, 3, 2, 1 after striking off the right-most digits successively i.e., if we remove 0, it is divisible by 9; if we remove 7290, it is divisible by 6 (that is, the number of digits remaining in the number) and so on.

3816547290 divisible by 10

381654729 divisible by 9

38165472 divisible by 8

3816547 divisible by 7

381654 divisible by 6

38165 divisible by 5

3816 divisible by 4

381 divisible by 3

38 divisible by 2

3 divisible by 1

Problem 3: Solution

There are two known solutions using all nine digits for

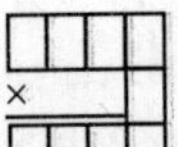

$1738 \times 4 = 6952$

$1963 \times 4 = 7852$

Given below are three more 1 to 9 series: the numbers are two and three times the first number respectively and the series uses 1 to 9 only once.

219, 438, 657

273, 546, 819

327, 654, 981

20

Mystifying 1729 and Ramanujan

Srinivasa Ramanujan, one of India's greatest mathematical geniuses, made substantial contributions to the analytical theory of numbers. He also worked on elliptic functions, continued fractions, and infinite series.

Ramanujan was born in Erode, a small village about 400 km southwest of Madras (now Chennai, India) in the year 1887 at his maternal grandparent's residence. He attended several different primary schools before finally settling down at the Town High School, Kumbakonam in January 1898. Ramanujan did well in all his school subjects and proved to be an all-round brilliant scholar. In 1900, when he was just thirteen, he began to work on geometric and arithmetic series.

He also made significant contributions to the development of partition functions and summation formulas involving constants such as π. A child prodigy, he was largely self-taught in mathematics and had compiled over 3,000 theorems by the year 1914 when he moved to Cambridge. Often, his formulae were stated without proof and were only later proven to be true. His results have inspired a large number of research and mathematical papers.

Ramanujan's achievements were recognised when on February 18, 1918, he was elected a fellow of the Cambridge Philosophical Society and then three days later, his name appeared on the list for election as a fellow of the Royal Society of London.

Ramanujan's home state of Tamil Nadu celebrates December 22 (Ramanujan's birthday) as 'State IT Day', honouring both the man, as a native of Tamil Nadu, and his achievements.

There is a famous anecdote related to Ramanujan which will introduce the number 1729 to you. This is what G. H. Hardy, the famous mathematician, had to say about Ramanujan:

> I remember once going to see (Ramanujan) when he was lying ill at Putney. I had ridden in taxicab number 1729 and remarked that the number seemed to me rather a dull one, and that I hoped it was not an unfavorable omen. 'No', he replied, '*it is a very interesting number; it is the smallest number expressible as the sum of two cubes in two different ways.*'

The two different ways are given below:

$$1729 = 1^3 + 12^3 = 9^3 + 10^3$$

Nowadays, any number which exhibits this property has been dubbed a *taxicab* number.

I also thought I would mention some facts which would prove of interest to the pure mathematician:

1. The number 1729 is the third Carmichael number (a Carmichael number, n, is a positive composite number which satisfies the congruence $b^{n-1} = 1 \pmod{n}$, where b and n are relatively prime to each other)
2. It is a Zeisel number (a Zeisel number is an integer, free of squares with at least three prime factors satisfying the equation $p_x = ap_{x-1} + b$, where a and b are constants).
3. It is a centred cube number, as well as a dodecagonal number (a number that can be represented by a 12-sided polygon), a 24-gonal and 84-gonal number.

Just one last thing about 1729.

$$1+7+2+9=19$$

$$19 \times 91 = 1729$$

Add up the digits, reverse the sum, multiply both and we get 1729 again !!

Ramanujan's constant, $e^{\pi\sqrt{163}}$, also has an interesting property. It is almost an integer.

$$e^{\pi\sqrt{163}} = 262,537,412,640,768,743.99999999999925...$$

What is surprising about this is that the mathematical constants e and π are transcendental numbers —they can never be the roots of finite equations with rational coefficients. Yet, here we have a combination of e and π that is almost an integer!

21

Līlāvatī

Bhāskaracārya otherwise known as *Bhāskara* is probably the most well-known mathematician of ancient India today. Bhāskara was born in 1114 CE according to a statement he recorded in one of his own works. He was from Bijjada Bida near the Sahyadri Mountains (the Western Ghats). Bijjada Bida is thought to be the present-day Bijapur in Mysore state, now the state of Karnataka, India. Bhāskara wrote his famous *Siddhānta Śiromaṇi* in the year 1150 CE. It is divided into four parts: *Līlāvatī* (arithmetic), *Bījagaṇita* (algebra), *Goladhyaya* (celestial globe), and *Gṛhagaṇita* (mathematics of the planets).

Here are two famous riddles from the *Līlāvatī*:

PROBLEM 1

O girl! Out of a group of swans, 7/2 times the square root of the number are playing on the shore of a tank. The two remaining ones are playing with amorous fight, in the water. What is the total number of swans?

PROBLEM 2

The woman's necklace broke.

A row of pearls mislaid.

One-sixth fell to the floor.

One-fifth upon the bed.

The young woman saved one-third of them.

One-tenth were caught by her lover.

If six pearls remained upon the string

How many pearls were there altogether?

Solution

PROBLEM 1: SOLUTION

The total number of swans is 16. Let x be the number of swans, thus

$$\frac{7}{2}\sqrt{x}+2=x,$$

or

$$x-2=\frac{7}{2}\sqrt{x}.$$

Squaring both sides we have,

$$x^2-4x+4=\frac{49}{4}x$$

$$x^2+4-\frac{65}{4}x=0.$$

Solving this we have,

$$x=16 \quad \text{or} \quad \frac{1}{4}.$$

Since the number of swans cannot be a fraction, there are 16 swans in the group.

PROBLEM 2: SOLUTION

There are 30 pearls in the women's necklace. Let x represent the original number of pearls on the necklace.

$$6+\left(\frac{x}{6}\right)+\left(\frac{x}{5}\right)+\left(\frac{x}{3}\right)+\left(\frac{x}{10}\right)=x$$

$$\left(\frac{6}{x}\right) + \frac{1}{6} + \frac{1}{5} + \frac{1}{3} + \frac{1}{10} = 1$$

$$\left(\frac{36}{x}\right) + 1 + \frac{6}{5} + 2 + \frac{3}{5} = 6$$

$$\left(\frac{180}{x}\right) + 15 + 9 = 30$$

$$\left(\frac{180}{x}\right) = 6$$

$$x = 30.$$

22

Amicable Numbers

Pythagoras, the famous Greek mathematician, was once asked, 'What is a friend?'. He replied that a friend is one 'who is the other "I" such as 220 and 284'. The numbers 220 and 284 form the smallest pair of amicable numbers (also known as friendly numbers) known to Pythagoras.

Why did Pythagoras consider the relationship between these numbers as a synonym to the relationship between friends? We can find this out from the definition: Two numbers are called amicable (or friendly) if each number is equal to the sum of the aliquot divisors (all the divisors excluding the number itself) of the other.

For example, the aliquot divisors of number 220 are 1, 2, 4, 5, 10, 11, 20, 22, 44, 55 and 110. The aliquot divisors of number 284 are 1, 2, 4, 71 and 142.

$$1 + 2 + 4 + 5 + 10 + 11 + 20 + 22 + 44 + 55 + 110 = 284$$

$$1 + 2 + 4 + 71 + 142 = 220$$

The smallest amicable pair (220, 284) has been known from antiquity and so much significance was attached to it that the possessor of one (it could be the digits of one's birthday), was assured of close friendship with the possessor of the other number of the pair. So much so, that in the past some marriages have been made on the basis of amicable numbers. Find out if 1210 and 1184 are amicable.

It was not until 1636 that the great Pierre de Fermat discovered another pair of amicable numbers (17296, 18416).

23

Bicycle with Square Wheels

'A bridge [...] is a very special thing. Haven't you seen how delicate they are in relation to their size? They soar like birds; they extend and embody our finest efforts; and they utilize the curve of heaven. When a catenary of steel a mile long is hung in the clear over a river, believe me, God knows. [...] the catenary, this marvelous graceful thing, this joy of physics, this perfect balance between rebellion and obedience, is God's own signature on earth. I think it pleases Him to see them raised.'

Mark Helprin, *Winter's Tale*

Suppose your bicycle had wheels which were square and not round—could you ever roll smoothly without jerks? A strange question—you would most probably answer 'no'. But there is a special kind of track on which a square wheel can move smoothly, *without any jerks*! The track has to be made of segments of catenaries like that shown in Figure 23.1.

Catenary is a word that most of us may not have heard unless we have something to do with transmission lines and railways. The name 'catenary' is associated with a curve because it describes the shape formed by a chain or rope freely suspended by its end points. It is actually from the Latin root, *catenareus*, for chain.

The word was developed from the correspondence between Leibniz and Huygens around 1690, but there seems to be some disagreement about who used the term first. Galileo believed that a freely hung rope formed a parabola. But this was disputed by the mathematician, Jungius (1587–1657).

Figure 23.1 *Bicycle with square wheels*

Mathematically speaking, the equation for the curve formed by a freely hung rope is

$$y = a\cosh(x/a).$$

So we can assume that the squarish-tyred cycle is a mathematical possibility. The only difficulty is that the track laying will be a nightmare for the civil engineer! Several types of polygons can be rolled jerk-free on tracks with segments of catenary, depending on the number of segments and their spacing (a special calculation has to be made for this). Figure 23.2 depicts this.

Observe in the figures, that the centre point of each polygon is moving in a straight line. You can also see that as the number of sides of the polygon increases, so does the number of segments of the catenary track. If you remember that a circle is a polygon with infinite sides, you will realise that the straight track can be considered as a special case of a catenary track—one with infinite segments.

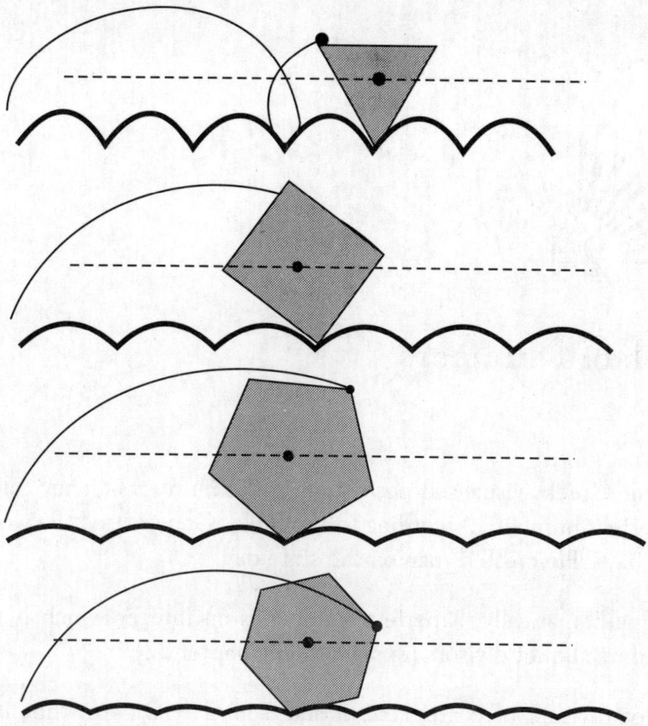

Figure 23.2 *Observe that the centre point of each polygon is moving in a straight line.*

24

Perfect Numbers

Ancient Greeks visualised perfection in the number 6. They called it a perfect number . According to the Bible, God created the world in six days; He created man on the sixth day.

But, mathematically, a perfect number is an integer which is the sum of its aliquot divisors (explained in Chapter 22).

Aliquot divisors of 6 are 1, 2, 3 and 1 + 2 + 3 = 6, thus it is a perfect number. The Ancient Greeks only knew the first four perfect numbers.

$$6 = 1 + 2 + 3$$

$$28 = 1 + 2 + 4 + 7 + 14$$

$$496 = 1 + 2 + 4 + 8 + 16 + 31 + 62 + 124 + 248$$

$$8128 = 1 + 2 + 4 + 8 + 16 + 32 + 64 + 127 + 254 + 508$$
$$+1016 + 2032 + 4064$$

Euclid discovered that the first four perfect numbers are generated by the formula $2^{n-1}(2n - 1)$.

$$\text{for } n = 2 : 2^1(2^2 - 1) = 6$$

$$\text{for } n = 3 : 2^2(2^3 - 1) = 28$$

for $n = 5 : 2^4(2^5 - 1) = 496$

for $n = 7 : 2^6(2^7 - 1) = 8128$

He also proved that the formula $2^{n-1}(2^n - 1)$ gives an even perfect number whenever $2^n - 1$ is prime. Do you see a relationship? The Mersenne prime (explained later, but for now, a Mersenne prime is one which can be expressed in the form, $2^n - 1$) comes into play. In order for $2^n - 1$ to be prime, it is necessary that n should be prime.

Something very unique about the perfect number is that it is the sum of all natural numbers up to $2^n - 1$. This follows from the general formula stating that the sum of the first m positive integers equals $(m^2 + m)/2$. Furthermore, any even perfect number except the first is the sum of the first $2^{(n-1)/2}$ odd cubes.

$$6 = 2^1(2^2 - 1) = 1 + 2 + 3$$

$$28 = 2^2(2^3 - 1) = 1 + 2 + 3 + 4 + 5 + 6 + 7 = 1^3 + 3^3$$

$$496 = 2^4(2^5 - 1) = 1 + 2 + 3 + ... + 29 + 30 + 31 = 1^3 + 3^3 + 5^3 + 7^3$$

$$8128 = 2^6(2^7 - 1) = 1 + 2 + 3 + ... + 125 + 126 + 127$$

$$= 1^3 + 3^3 + 5^3 + 7^3 + 9^3 + 11^3 + 13^3 + 15^3$$

I would like to point out just one more interesting fact about perfect numbers. Reciprocals of the divisors of a perfect number add up to 2.

For 6, we have

$$\frac{1}{6} + \frac{1}{3} + \frac{1}{2} + \frac{1}{1} = 2$$

For 28, we have

$$\frac{1}{28} + \frac{1}{14} + \frac{1}{7} + \frac{1}{4} + \frac{1}{2} + \frac{1}{1} = 2$$

25

Numbers in the Bible

I had heard that the worship of God is the prime stimulus to creativity. Even the most brilliant of scientists believed in a Supreme Being—this is not to say that they were religious in the 'blind' sense of the word, believing in mindless rituals and hours of praying in the aisle. The Church and the Bible also fascinated me, for the sheer architectural grandeur of its many churches and the noble values embodied in the religion itself. When I read the Bible, I looked at it from a mathematician's point of view. I tried to find some pattern in all the numbers used in the Bible.

The number 'one' signifies absolute singleness.

The number 'two' indicates witness and support. The Ten Commandments were written on two stones. Jesus's disciples were sent out in twos.

The number 'three' is mentioned numerous times in the Bible. It is a number signifying unity and accomplishment. The human race is traced to Noah's three sons. Jesus's earthly ministry lasted three years; he rose from the dead on the third day; and the Holy Trinity is three Divine Persons in one God.

'Six' is the number pertaining to man. Man was created on the sixth day. The Israelites caused the fall of Jericho by marching around its walls six times. Although, St Augustine (354–430 CE) writes in his famous text, *The City of God*,

> Six is a number perfect in itself, and not because God created all things in six days; rather, the converse is true. God created all things in six days because the number is perfect . . .

'Eight' is the number signifying new beginnings. During Noah's time, eight people were saved from the Flood. Circumcision was to be performed on the eighth day.

The Damned Triplicate 666

The number 666 is the number of the Antichrist (explained in Chapter 17). It is also known as the damned triplicate. Six is known as an 'imperfect number' (I know its confusing—just in Chapter 24, we mentioned that 6 was a perfect number. Well, it is mathematically, but in the Bible, it just does not reach perfection) because it is one short of seven, the 'perfect number' (seven days in the week taken to create the world, seven tongues of flame, seven spiritual gifts . . .). The number 666 has three sixes and three is the number of the Trinity, so 666 is seen as extremely imperfect. Therefore, 666 represents imperfect man, although mostly the Antichrist, while 777 represents God.

Some interesting properties of this number are

$$666 = 2^2 + 3^2 + 5^2 + 7^2 + 11^2 + 13^2 + 17^2$$

$$666 = 1 + 2 + 3 + 4 + 567 + 89$$

$$= 123 + 456 + 78 + 9$$

$$= 9 + 87 + 6 + 543 + 21$$

Three different ways to obtain 666 by using 1 to 9 and that too sequentially!

$$666 = (6^1 + 6^1 + 6^1) + (6^3 + 6^3 + 6^3)$$

Incredibly, the number 666 is equal to the sum of the digits of its 47th power, and is also equal to the sum of the digits of its 51st power. That is,

$$
\begin{aligned}
666^{47} = {} & 5049969684420796753173148798405564772941 51\\
& 629526540818811763266893654044661603306865\\
& 302888989271885967029756328621959466590473\\
& 3945856
\end{aligned}
$$

$$
\begin{aligned}
666^{51} = {} & 993540757591385940334263511341295980723858 6\\
& 374694310089971206913134607132829675825302 3\\
& 455821491848096074897283890063763421569409 7\\
& 683599029436416
\end{aligned}
$$

In fact, 666 is the only integer greater than one with this property. Also note that from the two powers, 47 and 51, we get $(4+7)(5+1) = 66$.

26

Kaprekar Numbers

The number 9999 is a Kaprekar number. Now you will be wondering what a Kaprekar number is.

A Kaprekar number is a special n digit number such that if it is squared, the sum of the squared quantity's right-most n digits and remaining part are equal to the number itself.

Take 9 for example

$$9^2 = 81 \text{ and } 8 + 1 = 9$$

Similarly,

$$703^2 = 494\,209, \text{ and } 494 + 209 = 703$$

Wonderful, isn't it!!!

Try out 500500.

The Kaprekar numbers were named after Shri Dattathreya Ramachandra Kaprekar (1905–1986) who discovered them.

Kaprekar was an Indian mathematician, whose name is associated with a number of concepts in number theory. He was born in Dahanu, near Mumbai, in India. Even as a small child, his passion was for numbers.

He never received a formal post-graduate training, but from 1930 until his retirement in 1962, he worked as a schoolteacher in Devlali, India. Kaprekar discovered many interesting properties in recreational number theory. He published extensively, writing about such topics as recurring decimals, magic squares , and integers with special properties.

Kaprekar also discovered an interesting operation, now known as the Kaprekar's operation.

First choose a four-digit number where the digits are all different (that is, not numbers like 1111, 2222, ...). Then re-arrange the digits to get the largest and smallest numbers these digits can make. Finally, subtract the smallest number from the largest to get a new number, and repeat the operation for each new number.

Let us try 2006.

$$6200 - 0026 = 6174$$

$$7641 - 1467 = 6174$$

6174 repeats itself. Very interesting!

Let us try 2005.

$$5200 - 0025 = 5175$$

$$7551 - 1557 = 5994$$

$$9954 - 4599 = 5355$$

$$5553 - 3555 = 1998$$

$$9981 - 1899 = 8082$$

$$8820 - 0288 = 8532$$

$$8532 - 2358 = 6174$$

$$7641 - 1467 = 6174$$

So this number 6174 is really unique and is true for all 4-digit numbers which have different digits. You can try some more.

Something that came to my mind and would have definitely struck a similar note in the reader's mind, was whether this is true for all numbers consisting of 2 digits, 3 digits etc. Well, there is no unique number for 2 digit numbers but for 3 digit numbers, the magic figure is 495.

Try 520.

$$520 - 025 = 495$$

Try 765.

$$765 - 567 = 198$$

$$981 - 189 = 792$$

$$972 - 279 = 693$$

$$963 - 369 = 594$$

$$954 - 459 = 495$$

again

$$954 - 459 = 495$$

It repeats itself.

Kaprekar published this article as 'Another solitaire game' in *Scripta Mathematica*, vol 15, pp 244–245 (1949).

7776 is another interesting number.

$7776^5 = 28430288029929701376$, dividing this is in five equal parts, we find

$$2843 + 0288 + 0299 + 2970 + 1376 = 7776.$$

27

Palindromes

Palindromes—words which spell the same backward and forward have been a source of attraction for linguists through the ages. An example of a palindrome is noon. Noon is not related, as we might be led to believe, to the number twelve, but to the number nine. It is derived from the Latin *nona* (ninth) and originally referred to the ninth hour after sunrise, which is closer to the present 3 PM.

In mathematics, palindromic numbers have also fascinated the number maniac. Some striking patterns can be conceived.

I got the following from Martin Gardner's *A Gardner's Workout*:

Think of a two-digit number. Reverse the digits (05 for 50) and add this number to the selected one. Repeat the steps till you get a palindrome.

Try 49.

$$49 + 94 = 143$$

Repeat the steps,

$$143 + 341 = 484$$

which is a palindrome!

This is true for almost all numbers—the iterative process of adding a number to the number obtained when its digits are reversed results in a palindrome.

Warning! Use a calculator for the addition as some numbers get very large. Try 89 for instance. Can you even guess what number is generated?

8813200023188!!

28

Weights and Lesser Weights

The problem of weighing substances using logic instead of physical means has thrilled several amateur mathematicians; but it has the potential to irritate the professional—finding a solution might be possible but proving why the solution works remains elusive most of the time. We present below some very interesting problems and their solutions. The reader is advised to stop and think over every problem, preferably with a rough paper and pen.

Hundred kilogrammes with five stones

If a grocer is to weigh 1 to 100 kg using only five stones, what should the weight of each stone be?

We can also state a variant to the problem: What should be the minimum number of stones and of what weight each, so that he is able to weigh 1 to 100 using the weights on *only one side of the balance*?

Five balls

Mr. Deep has a set of five balls, identical in touch and appearance. But none of them have similar weights. He has to arrange the balls in order of weight from the heaviest to the lightest. At his disposal is a balance with no weighing blocks. What is the minimum number of weighings required for this?

HINT: Seven

Nine grammes out of twenty four

In a bag there are 24 g of nails. Can you measure out 9 g using a balance with two pans?

Counterfeit coins

Mr. Pal has 101 coins. He is told that 50 of them are counterfeit and differ by 1 gramme from the genuine coins. He has a scale with two pans, which can show the difference in weight between two sets of objects placed in each pan.

He chooses one coin. How is he to know whether it is counterfeit or not?

Lighter golf ball

A golfer bought ten bags of golf balls. It was later discovered that one of the bags contained balls lighter by 1 gramme. Using only one weighing on a digital balance, find out the culprit bag. The weight of each ball is 10 g.

Variant to the golfer's problem

Suppose the golfer regularly buys golf balls in packs of six. He suspects that the dealer is cheating him by including one box of sub-standard balls in a set of ten boxes. The sub-standard balls were the same in size and appearance as the normal ball, *only a gramme lighter*.

Once after receiving a set of ten boxes with six balls in each box, he decided to find out the faulty box. He only has a pair of scales and a set of weights; he does not know the weight of a normal golf ball. Can he determine the faulty box in just one weighing?

The following is by far the best logical problem I have ever solved.

The one out of thirteen defective ball problem

You have a balance with two pans but no weights. There are 13 balls, which are identical in size and shape. But one of them is defective—*it is lighter or heavier than the rest* (please note this carefully otherwise like most, you would shout 'Eureka!', being miles away from the solution).

The problem is to find out the odd ball in just three weighings.

HINT Label the balls 1 to 13 and form groups of four. This is not the only way but certainly the easiest.

The fourteen coin problem

In a set of 14 coins exactly 7 coins are counterfeit and weigh less than the genuine coins. How can we differentiate all the counterfeit and genuine coins in only three weighings?

This is left unsolved. But it definitely has a solution, unknown to author.

Discussion and solutions

Hundred kilogrammes with five stones

Using both sides of the balance, he needs just 1, 3, 9, 27 and 81 kg weights. This is a special property of base 3 numbers.

Suppose he had to weigh 25 kg, the 27 kg and 1 kg weights would be placed on one side and the 3 kg block along with the item on the other. Thus he has

$$27 + 1 - 3 = 25 \text{ kg.}$$

Similarly for 100 kg, he has to place the 81 kg, 27 kg and 1 kg weights on one side and the 9 kg weight on the other, to have

$$81 + 27 + 1 = 109 \text{ and } 109 - 9 = 100 \text{ kg!}$$

The variant to the problem

In the variant to the problem, we have to use only one side of the pan. Here the special property of the base 2 is used. The least number of weights required are 7 and the weights are 1, 2, 4, 8, 16, 32 and 64.

Suppose you were to weigh 25 kg, you would have to use the 16, 8 and 1 kg weights.

To get 100 kg, you would need the 64, 32 and 4 kg weights. You can calculate similarly for all the units between 1 and 100.

Five balls

1. Weigh any two balls. Label them H and L.
2. Weigh any two from the remaining three balls. Label them h and l.
3. Now weigh H with h. Re-designate whichever is heavier as H and the other ball as h. Put L aside and have H, h, l in order.
4. In the 4th and 5th weighings, it is possible to place the fifth ball in order among H, h, l.
5. In the 6th and 7th weighings (done regardless of the placement of the fifth ball), the ball designated L can be placed using the fact that L is lighter than H.

NOTE Steps 4 and 5 have been purposefully kept imprecise for you to try it out yourself and appreciate the logic. Try hard.

Nine grammes out of twenty four

Use the balance to divide 24 g into 12 g each. Then divide the 12 g into two equal parts of 6 g. Keep one part aside. Now divide 6 g into two parts of 3 g each. Take on part of this and put the 6 g heap on one side of the pans. Now you can measure 9 g. Simple!

Counterfeit coins

Lay aside the chosen coin. Divide the remaining coins in two piles of 50 coins each. If the chosen coin is genuine then the difference in weights of the two piles will be even, otherwise odd. The logic is too good to be explained, try it yourself.

Lighter golf ball

Take 1 ball from the first bag, 2 from the second and so on until the tenth bag with 10 balls.

The total number of balls is 55; the correct weight should be 550 g. After determining the weight of the set of balls, it can easily be identified which bag is defective.

For example 545 g would mean 5 balls are defective and five balls were taken from the fifth bag.

Variant to the golfer's problem

1. Label the boxes A to J.
2. Take 1 ball from A, 2 from B, 3 from C, 4 from D, 5 from E, and place them on the left pan of the scales.
3. Again take 1 ball from F, 2 from G, 3 from H, 4 from I and 5 from J, and place them on the right pan of the scales.
4. Using the weights, balance the scales. The number of grammes required, and the side of the scale which requires it, determines the faulty box.

For example, if 4 g were needed on the left pan, it would mean 4 balls are lighter in one of the boxes A–E, and 4 balls had been taken from box D. So D is the faulty box. If H had been the faulty box, then 3 g would be required on the right side.

The one out of thirteen defective ball problem

This is the best logical problem you can solve, so try once more before looking at the solution.

First, number the balls from 1 to 13 and group them as (1, 2, 3, 4); (5, 6, 7, 8); (9, 10, 11, 12); keep 13 aside. Let L denote the left side of the balance and R denote the right.

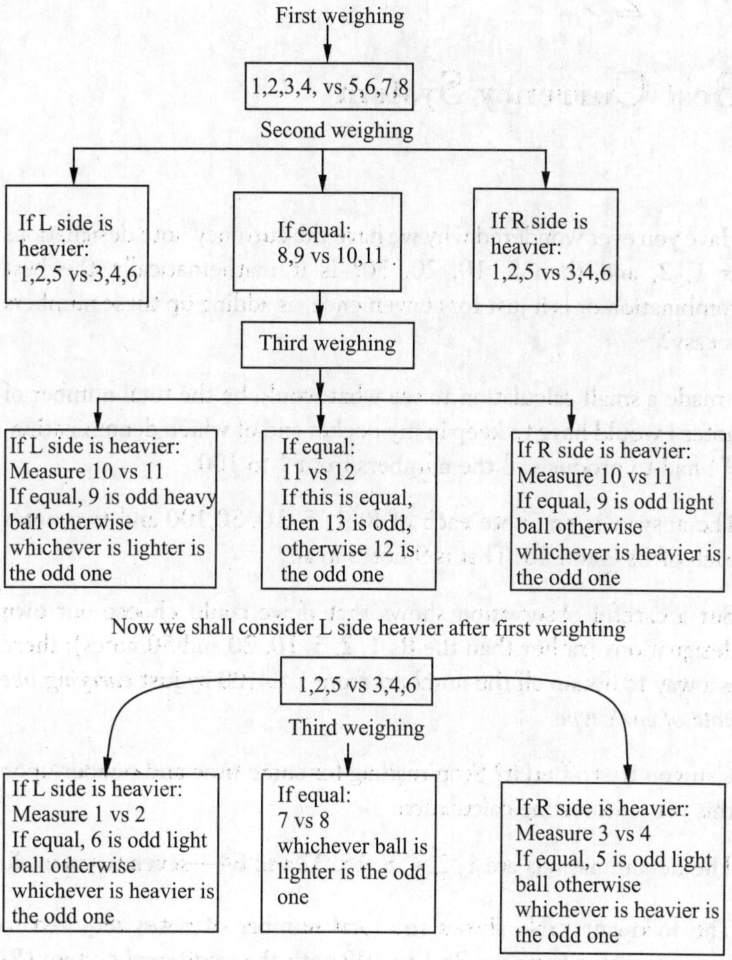

The R side heavier case after first weighing can be solved using the same logical sequence of weighing

29

Best Currency System

Have you ever wondered why we have the currency note designations as 1, 2, and then 5, 10, 20, 50? Is it mathematically the best combination or is it just for convenience, as adding up these numbers is easy?

I made a small calculation to see what would be the total number of notes I would have to keep in my pocket and of which denomination, if I had to produce all the numbers from 1 to 100.

The answer is one note each of Rs 1, 5, 10, 50,100 and two notes each of Rs 2 and 20. That is 9 notes in all.

But a careful observation shows that if we could choose our own designations (rather than the Rs 1, 2, 5, 10, 20 and 50 notes), there is a way to obtain all the numbers from 1 to 100 by just *carrying one note of each type*.

Can you try to find it? Stop reading for some time and ponder upon this very interesting calculation.

The denominations are 1, 2, 4, 8, 16, 32 and 64—seven notes in all.

The following table shows the total number of notes required to have any value between Rs 1 to 100 with the traditional system (Rs 1, 2, 5, 10, 20 and 50 notes) and the system I worked out (Rs 1, 2, 4, 8, 16, 32 and 64). An exercise for you is to discover how we got these values.

Currency	New	Old
1	1	1
2	1	1
3	2	2
4	1	2
5	2	1
6	2	2
7	3	2
8	1	3
9	2	3
10	2	1
11	3	2
12	2	2
13	3	3
14	3	3
15	4	2
16	1	3
17	2	3
18	2	4
19	3	4
20	2	1
21	3	2
22	3	2
23	4	3
24	2	3
25	3	2
26	3	3
27	4	3
28	3	4
29	4	4
30	4	2
31	5	3
32	1	3
33	2	4
34	2	4
35	3	3
36	3	4
37	4	4
38	3	5
39	4	5

Currency	New	Old
40	2	2
41	3	3
42	3	3
43	4	4
44	3	4
45	4	3
46	4	4
47	5	4
48	2	5
49	3	5
50	3	1
51	4	2
52	3	2
53	4	3
54	4	3
55	5	2
56	3	3
57	4	3
58	4	4
59	5	4
60	4	2
61	5	3
62	5	3
63	6	4
64	1	4
66	2	4
67	3	4
68	2	5
69	3	5
70	3	2
71	4	3
72	2	3
73	3	4
74	3	4
75	4	3
76	3	4
77	4	4
78	4	5
79	5	5

Currency	New	Old
80	2	3
81	3	4
82	3	4
83	4	5
84	3	5
85	4	4
86	4	5
87	5	5
88	3	6
89	4	6

Currency	New	Old
90	4	3
91	5	4
92	4	4
93	5	5
94	5	5
95	6	4
96	2	5
97	3	5
99	3	6
100	3	1

The total number of notes required with the present traditional system is 341 and with the new mathematically correct system it is 320.

But try getting Rs 50 with the new system,

$$50 = 32 + 16 + 2$$

It is a bit inconvenient compared to just a Rs 50 note. The adding up would also take a little getting used to. Anyway, all this is to be taken only as a mathematical recreation. The present system is the best!!

Again my obsession leads me to a problem. Is there no simpler way with lesser denominations to have—say, only four currency notes? Various combinations were tried but finally, using a computer programme, the four denominations using the least number of notes to produce Rs 1 to 100 was found to be 1, 5, 18 and 25. There is no precondition of using them only once. Try figuring it out. The only clue I will give you is that the total number of notes required is 393!

30

Why the Decimal System?

The answer, I guess, is obvious. We have 10 fingers on our hands and fingers are the first things we use (so must have the early humans) to calculate or count. Thus there is no doubt that base 10 is the most convenient counting system. True, but then why are there so many other base systems across ages, cultures and geographical locations? Good question.

The origins of our modern decimal or the base 10 number system can be traced back to ancient Egyptian, Babylonian (Sumerian), and Chinese roots. But the real credit for the base 10 system with a symbol for zero goes to the Hindu mathematicians of the fifth and sixth centuries. After their discovery of the system it was transmitted to mathematicians in the Islamic world who, during the period from the 9th to the 11th centuries CE developed it to include decimal fractions. The introduction of this system in the West took place with the translation of Muhammad ibn Mūsa al-Khwārizmī's (c.780–850) treatise in the twelfth century.

The art of reckoning (*ganita*) was held in the highest esteem by the ancient Indians. They used symbols for marks or divisions (*ankas*) which are the ancestors of the modern decimal digits (1, 2, 3, 4, 5, 6, 7, 8, 9). The introduction of a tenth symbol for zero (0) paved the way to the *positional system* of decimal numeration. The Sanskrit name for zero is *shoonya* ('void', 'nothingness' or 'emptiness').

Before its invention, the need for *zero* was circumvented in India, as it had been everywhere else. The ancient Indians used different Sanskrit words for all the successive powers of ten.

Indeed, the place value system of enumeration was built into the Sanskrit language. Any large number was expressed as first naming the largest power of ten possible in the number taken along with a non-*zero* anka (from 1 to 9) (the rest of the integer, if any, being named using the same scheme recursively).

About 2000 years ago, it occurred to an extraordinary Indian that the powers of ten need not be mentioned at all, *provided* a symbol is unambiguously given for each power of ten. This symbol took the form of a small circle with a centre dot. Thus zero was born. As time went by the centre dot was dropped to give rise to the modern '0'and the modern decimal system.

The oldest surviving reference to this modern decimal system is a sacred text called *Agni Purana*. The new system was used (with the multiplication tables) shortly thereafter in Roman Syria (modern Jordan) by Nicomachus of Gerasa (CE 60–20) in his famous *Arithmetike Eisagoge* (Introduction to Arithmetic). Arithmetic as a field of study separate from geometry was established through this work.

31

Binary is Okay But Why Hexadecimal in Computers?

The digits 0 and 1 are perhaps the most familiar figures for all computer literates and semi-literates. It is also common knowledge that they depict the 'off' and 'on' condition respectively. Those of us who venture just a bit more into the computer world would have encountered the hexadecimal system —the base 16 numbers. But why use such a strange and complex number system which uses 0 to 9 and then the first six alphabets A B C D E F? Let us learn a little bit more about the system before we get into this. Letters are used for the numbers from ten through fifteen

A = 10; B = 11; C = 12; D = 13; E = 14; F = 15

They can either be in upper case or lower case. A typical operation in base 16 will look like:

```
  3F2
 +B37
 ----
  F29
```

To interpret such numbers as base 10 numbers, one needs to know the powers of 16.

$$16^3 = 4096$$
$$16^2 = 256$$
$$16^1 = 16$$
$$16^0 = 1$$

So the number F29 in base 16 is equal to $(F \times 16^2) + (2 \times 16^1) + (9 \times 16^0)$ which is calculated as,

$$\begin{array}{rcr} 15 \times 256 & = & 3840 \\ 2 \times 16 & = & 32 \\ 9 \times 1 & = & 9 \\ \hline & & 3881 \text{ in base } 10 \end{array}$$

Difficult indeed, but a simple property makes it a very straightforward system to operate in—it is easy to change numbers from base 16 to base 2 and back.

Every digit of the hexadecimal number can be broken down into a 4-digit binary number. These numbers are then written down in the same order as the hexadecimal number and we have got the equivalent binary (base 2) number.

Let us consider the same example of F29.

F is equal to 15 which is 8 + 4 + 2 + 1 (these are the powers of 2).

That means that $F = (1 \times 2^3) + (1 \times 2^2) + (1 \times 2^1) + (1 \times 2^0)$.

So $F_{16} = 1111_2$ (the subscripts show the base).

Since 2_{16} is (1×2^1), then $2_{16} = 0010_2$

Since 9_{16} is $(1 \times 2^3(8)) + (1 \times 2^0)$, then $9_{16} = 1001_2$

Putting this together makes $F29_{16} = 1111\ 0010\ 1001_2$.

To switch between base 2 and base 16 one only needs to learn to write the numbers 0 to 15 in base 2.

When expressing large numbers, the binary system is very inefficient, as is any low base system. Higher base systems can express numbers using fewer characters. To illustrate this, we will look at a table showing numbers as they would look in different base systems. The columns are different systems: base 2, 3, 4, 8, 9, 10, 16, and 18. The rows are different numbers as they look in each system.

Base							
2	**3**	**4**	**8**	**9**	**10**	**16**	**18**
10	2	2	2	2	2	2	2
1,000	22	20	10	8	8	8	8
11,011	1,000	123	33	30	27	1B	19
1,100,100	10,201	1,210	144	121	100	64	5A
100,000,000	100,111	10,000	400	314	256	100	E4
1,000,000,000	200,222	20,000	1000	628	512	200	1A8

NOTE The commas are present only to simplify reading

Notice that it is much simpler to express numbers using larger base systems. Because computers rely on the binary system, base 16 is used for expressing long binary numbers. There is another reason why the base 16 is used as an auxiliary for the binary system instead of say 10, or 18.

If you look at the table, you will see that 100,000,000 in the binary system is 100 in the hexadecimal system, whereas it is 256 in base 10 and E4 in base 18. Thus the equivalent numbers are easier to deal with. The hexadecimal system is very compatible with the binary system because 16 is a power of 2. This is the same reason why base 4 and 8 are also very nice systems to represent binary numbers.

This is not only applicable with powers of 2 though. All of the base 3 numbers in the table work well with base 9 (though the only number in the table showing this obviously is '1000'). One thing to note is that base 10 is not 'nice' with respect to base 2, and base 18 is not 'nice' with respect to base 3, though each is a multiple of the latter.

In order for number systems to 'look good together', the higher system must be a power of the lower.

What does this all mean?

Conversion between binary and hexadecimal numbers is easy. We simply club the binary digits in groups of four, starting from the least significant bit, and translate them into hexadecimal numbers (inserting leading zeroes in front if the need is felt). The following examples will clarify this statement.

Base 10	Base 2	Base 16
1	0001	1
10	1010	A
100	0110 0100	64
1,000	0011 1110 1000	3E8
10,000	0010 0111 0001 0000	2710
100,000	0001 1000 0110 1010 0000	186A0
1,000,000	1111 0100 0010 0100 0000	F4240

The binary system is an effective number system for computers because it is easy to implement it with digital electronics. But humans find the binary system very inefficient as it requires so many digits to represent a single number. For example, the number 76 takes only two digits to write in decimal, yet seven digits are required to write it in binary (1001100). To overcome this limitation, the hexadecimal number system was developed.

The base 16 numbering system is used as a shorthand for representing binary numbers. Each half byte (four bits) is assigned a hex digit. Hex values are identified with an h or a dollar sign, thus $3E0, 3E0h and 3E0H all stand for the hex number 3E0.

Thus hexadecimal numbers can represent every byte (8 bits) as two consecutive digits and is easier for humans to read. Yet the wonder of it is that it still retains the digital nature of computers.

32

HCF and LCM

The concept of LCM and HCF is probably the most confusing of all mathematical concepts. To readers who remember anything in high school mathematics, this would be the last thing they can recall correctly. Try to calculate the LCM for 20 and 48.

Let us try to make it simple. LCM—least common multiple—is the least multiple which can be obtained after multiplying any number in the set with some other number.

For example, consider the set of numbers 20 and 24.

The factors are

$$20 = 2 \times 2 \times 5$$

$$24 = 2 \times 2 \times 2 \times 3$$

so the LCM is 120 as it is the least number which is a multiple of 20 and 24.

Now coming to HCF—the highest common factor—it is the highest factor (divisor) which can divide all the numbers in a set without a remainder.

Let us consider 20 and 24. They are both divisible by 2 and 4, but 4 is the highest common divisor. Let us take a more complex example.

Consider the set 48, 60,120. Here 2, 3, 4, 6 and 12 all divide the three numbers but 12 is the highest among them.

Interestingly,

$$\text{HCF} \times \text{LCM} = \text{product of the numbers.}$$

How are these concepts useful in arithmetic and algebra? Consider the following problems.

PROBLEM 1

The length and breadth of a room are 3 metres and 2 metres respectively. What will be the size of the square tile if its floor is to be covered fully with a minimum number of square tiles of the same size without breaking them?

PROBLEM 2

There are two sections A and B of a certain class in a school. The children of Section A organise a quiz competition after every 15 days and those of Section B after every 20 days. If both sections organise it together on the first day of the session, after how many days will they organise it together again?

The concepts of HCF and LCM are used here.

PROBLEM 1: SOLUTION

The size of the tile should be the highest number that divides completely both 3 and 2, i.e., the HCF of 3 and 2, which is 1. So the size of the square tile should be 1m by 1m.

Suppose the room was of dimensions 6 m by 4 m, square tiles of 2 m by 2 m would completely cover the room without breaking any tile as HCF of 6 and 4 is 2.

PROBLEM 2: SOLUTION

In this case the number of days would be the least number that is a multiple of both 15 and 20, i.e., LCM of 15 and 20.

$$15 = 5 \times 3$$

$$20 = 4 \times 5, \text{ thus LCM} = 3 \times 4 \times 5 = 60$$

So after exactly 60 days they would be organising the event together again.

33

Power of Indices, Reaching the Moon and the Inventor of Chess

Some of the most intriguing problems and facts came to light after we learnt the power of 'powers', i.e., indices, laws of exponents.

If you were to reach the moon by folding a strip of paper (of say 0.1 mm thickness), how many times would you have to fold the paper?

The moon is roughly 3.85×10^8 m from the earth—not much really, just 3,85,000 km.

Per fold, the thickness of paper doubles i.e., after the first fold it becomes

$$0.1 \times 2 = 0.2 \text{ mm}$$

Distance to the moon = 3,85,00,00,00,000 mm

Let n be the number of folds required to reach the moon. Then

$$2^n \times 0.1 = 3,85,00,00,00,000 \text{ mm}$$

Using logarithms, n is calculated to be approximately 42.

Unbelievable! Only 42 folds of a 0.1 mm thick paper are required to reach the moon!

I will end this section with an exercise for you.

The sun is about 150000000 km from the earth, how many folds will be required (using paper of the same thickness) to reach the sun?

Inventor of chess

Centuries ago, there was a ruler who loved games—the more challenging, the better. Any one who invented a new and interesting game was rewarded immensely. It was at this time that a very intelligent mathematician invented the game of chess and presented it to the ruler. The ruler was so amused by the game that he granted the mathematician a wish—he could ask for anything he wanted. Remember the mathematician was very intelligent. He thought for a while and then said:

I am a simple man, not interested in glory, mansions or lots of money. I just need to feed myself. So, my dear Lord, all I ask is that you grant me enough grains of wheat to fit the chess board . . .

The ruler was taken aback, "That's all! Come on, you are insulting me!"

"No, my Lord I have not completed my request. But please promise me that you will honour your commitment."

"Yes, of course", replied the ruler.

"Alright. I would like you to place one grain on the first square of the board, two on the second, four on the third and so on, doubling the number of grains on each square till the 64th square. I will be satisfied with this amount."

The ruler was amused but much to his dismay, he could not keep his commitment. It would have been impossible.

STOP. Do not read further. Try figuring out why? In case you get bogged down, read ahead.

The number of grains the ruler would have to place on the 64th square is 2^{63} (2 raised to the 63rd power).

The total number of grains on the board would be $2^{64} - 1$.

These facts can be easily deduced by considering just the first few squares, and generalising your findings. A proof can also be found using mathematical induction or the geometric series.

$$2^{64} - 1 = 18,446,744,073,709,551,615$$

That happens to be much more wheat than exists in the whole world. In fact, it would probably just fit in a warehouse 40 km long, 40 km wide, and 300 m high.

34

Instant Cube Root: Mathemagic

Cube roots up to 6 digits

What is the cube root of 262144?

Seems like a hard problem to solve without a calculator or a pen and paper. But here is a superb way to dazzle your friends with your astonishing calculation ability.

The cube root of any 6-digit number has to be less than 100, so you could consider memorising the first 100 cubes.

Divide the number into two parts; it would help to put a separator after the first three digits 262,144.

The left part 262 is between $216 = 6^3$ and $343 = 7^3$. This means 262144 lies somewhere between $216000 = 60^3$ and $343000 = 70^3$. Hence the answer is surely between 60 and 70.

Something very special about cubes of single digits is that the last digit is unique. To understand what I mean, let us see the following table. The second row numbers are the cubes of the respective first row numbers.

1	2	3	4	5	6	7	8	9
1	8	27	64	125	216	343	512	729

So all you have to know—rather remember very definitely—is these cubes and the associated last digit which is unique. For 1,4,5,6 and 9, the cube root is the same as the last digit of the cube. For the pairs (3, 7) and (2, 8), the last digits are the same as the other member of the pair.

Applying this to our cube 262144, it is not a tough task at all to find the cube root (after a few minutes of practice). With experience, in just 15 seconds, the answer 64 will emerge, amazing all your friends.

Let us try finding the cube root of another 6-digit number, say 571787. You might be able to answer this in 10 seconds now—83.

As 571 is between 512 and 729, the first digit of the cube root is 8. Since 7 is the last digit associated with the cube of 3, we have 3 as the second digit.

There are many very interesting ways to find cube roots using unconventional methods, but this one is perfect for showing off, as it involves absolutely no calculations and is actually mental.

35

Calculating the Size of the Earth: Trigonometrical Potentialities

Since its earliest days, geometry has been applied to practical problems of measurement—whether to find the height of a pyramid, or the area of a field, or the size of the earth. The word 'geometry' is derived from the Greek word *geo* (earth) and *metron* (to measure). But the ambition of the early Greek scientists went even farther than measuring the earth—using simple geometry and later trigonometry, they attempted to estimate the size of the *universe*.

In the year 240 BCE, Eratosthenes, a famous Greek scientist achieved the feat for which he is chiefly remembered—computing the size of the earth.

It was known that at noon on the day of the summer solstice (the longest day of the year), the sun's rays directly illuminated the bottom of a deep well in the town of Syene (now Aswan) in Upper Egypt. The sun was exactly overhead at noon as Aswan lies on the Tropic of Cancer. The shadow of a vertical rod in Alexandria, due north of Syene, showed that the sun was about 7.2 degrees from the zenith, about one-fiftieth of a full circle (360°).

Eratosthenes very rightly assumed that the sun is so far away from the earth that its rays reach us practically parallel. Hence the difference in the sun's elevation as seen from the two locations must be due to the *sphericity of the earth*. Since the distance between Alexandria and Syene was 5,000 stadia (as measured by the time it took the king's messengers to run between the two cities), the circumference of the earth must be fifty times this distance, or 250,000 stadia.

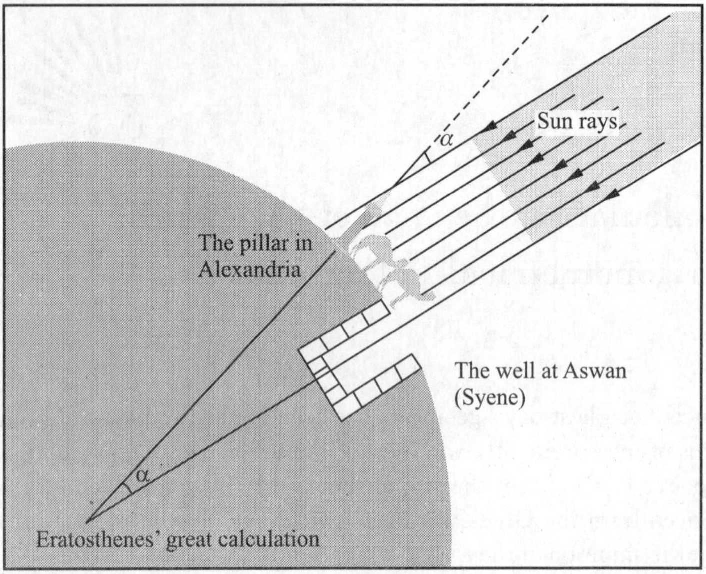

Eratosthenes' great calculation

The exact length of the stadium, the geographical distance unit in the Greek era, is not known; estimates vary from 607 to 738 feet, the smaller figure referring to the Roman stadium of later use. The circumference of the earth as found by Eratosthenes is therefore between 29,000 and 35,000 miles. The correct value is amazingly close—24,818 miles for the polar circumference and 24,902 miles for the equatorial. Eratosthenes used the science of geometry in its literal sense: to measure the earth.

Barnabas Hughes, in his Introduction to *Regiomontanus on Triangles* said:

> It is quite difficult to describe with certainty the beginning of trigonometry. In general, one may say that the emphasis was placed first on astronomy, then shifted to spherical trigonometry, and finally moved on to plane trigonometry.

Now we will try to answer a basic query—how did this word 'sine' originate?

There are several stories, told in different ways, but what is found to be most authentic is an early Hindu work on astronomy, the *Surya Siddhanta*. This work gives a table of half-chords based on Ptolemy's table of chords (a table of sines for every angle up to 90° in quarter degree intervals).

The sine as a function of an angle was first described in the *Aryabhatiya* of Aryabhata (ca. CE 510), considered the earliest Hindu treatise on pure mathematics. In this work, Aryabhata II (also known as Aryabhata the elder; born 475 or 476, died ca. 550) uses the word *ardha-jya* for the half-chord which was shortened to *jya* or *jiva*.

The etymological journey of the modern word 'sine' is interesting and starts from here. When the Arabs translated the *Aryabhatiya* into their own language, they retained the word *jiva* without translating its meaning. In Arabic and Hebrew, words consist mostly of consonants, the pronunciation of the missing vowels being understood through common usage. Thus *jiva* could also be pronounced as *jiba* or *jaib*. In Arabic *jaib* means bosom, fold, or bay.

When the Arabic version was translated into Latin, *jaib* was translated into *sinus*, which also means bosom, bay, or curve. Soon the word *sinus* or *sine* in its English version became common in mathematical texts throughout Europe. The abbreviated notation 'sin' was first used by Edmund Gunter (1581–1626), an English minister who later became professor of astronomy at Gresham College in London. In 1624 he invented a mechanical device, the 'Gunter scale' for computing with logarithms—a forerunner of the familiar slide rule —and the notation 'sin' (as well as tan) first appeared in a drawing describing his invention.

The remaining five trigonometric functions have a more recent history. The cosine function, which we regard today as equal in importance to the sine, first arose from the need to compute the sine of the complementary angle. Aryabhata called it *kotijya*. The name *cosinus* originated with Edmund Gunter: he wrote co sinus, which was later modified to cosinus by John Newton (1622–1678), a teacher and author of mathematics textbooks (he is unrelated to Isaac Newton) in 1658. The abbreviated notation 'cos' was first used in 1674 by Sir Jonas Moore (1617–1679), an English mathematician and surveyor.

The functions 'secant' and 'cosecant' came into being even later.

The word 'tangent' comes from the Latin word *tangere* (to touch). Its association with the tangent function may have come from the fact that the tangent to a circle is related to this function on the unit circle.

Trigonometry has opened many doors for humanity. In other words:

> The science of trigonometry was in a sense a precursor of the telescope. It brought faraway objects within the compass of measurement and first made it possible for man to penetrate in a quantitative manner the far reaches of space.
>
> Stanley L. Jaki, *The Relevance of Physics* (1966).

36

Sequences and Series

Carl Friedrich Gauss, the great German mathematician, was in elementary school when his teacher asked the class to find the sum of the first 100 natural numbers. While the rest of the class was struggling with the problem, Gauss had the answer in no time.

He used the formula for calculating the sum of n terms of an arithmetic progression (AP)—the sum of the first n terms in an AP is n times the average of the first and the last term in the AP

Arithmetic progression, what is this new term? It is a series of numbers such that there is a constant difference between successive terms. For example, consider the AP 2, 5, 8, ... Here the difference between the first and the second term; the second and the third term and so on is 3.

The sum of an AP series is given by the formula,

$$S_n = \frac{n \times (2a + (n-1)d)}{2}, \text{ where}$$

S_n = sum of series

a = first term of the series

d = constant difference

n = number of terms

There is another very useful and interesting series of numbers called geometric progression or GP in short. The successive terms in this case have a constant ratio i.e., ratio of the second term with the first term is equal to the ratio of the last term with the second last term. For example, 2, 6, 18, 54,. . .. Here the ratio of successive terms is 3.

The sum of a GP is given by the formula

$$S_n = \frac{a(1-r^n)}{1-r}, \text{ for } r<1 \text{ and } \frac{a(r^n-1)}{r-1}, \text{ for } r>1$$

where,

S_n = sum of series

a = first term of the series

r = constant ratio

n = number of terms

Using these formulae some very intuitive solutions can be found for various series of numbers. For example, can you find the sum, up to n terms, of the series,

$$9, 99, 999, 9999, 99999, \ldots, \ldots, \ldots$$

At first glance there seems to be no easy way, but wait. Think a while and then proceed.

This is not a GP, but it can be converted to one like this

$$10, 100-1, 1000-1, 10000-1, \ldots \text{ or}$$

$$10-1, 10^2-1, 10^3-1, 10^4-1, \ldots, 10^n-1$$

Thus, $S_n = (10 + 10^2 + 10^3 + \ldots n \,\text{terms}) - (1 + 1 + 1 + \ldots n \,\text{times})$

Using the formula for GP given above,

$$S_n = \frac{10(10^n-1)}{10-1} - n = \frac{10(10^n-1)}{9} - n$$

Here r, the common ratio, is 10 and a, the first term, is also 10.

Such series find application in physics, chemistry, biology, etc, to simplify various calculations.

Recurring decimals can also be expressed as a geometric series. Here is an exciting explanation.

Consider the recurring decimal 0.33333333 . . .. This can be written as,

$$0.333333 = 0.3 + 0.03 + 0.003 + 0.0003 + \ldots \infty.$$

Observe the right-hand side of the equation carefully. This can be perceived as a GP with

first term $a = 0.3$,

common ratio $r = 0.1$ and

number of terms $n = \infty$

Using these values in the formula for $r < 1$,

$$S_n = \frac{a(1 - r^n)}{1 - r}.$$

We have r^n approaching zero since any number less than one raised to the power of infinity is zero. Therefore the formula reduces to

$$S_n = \frac{a}{1 - r}.$$

Inserting the values in this formula, we get

$$\text{Sum} = \frac{0.3}{1 - 0.1} = \frac{1}{3}.$$

Great! Wasn't that easy!

Did you know that

$$3^{1/2} \times 3^{1/4} \times 3^{1/8} \times 3^{1/16} \ldots\ldots = 3.$$

It does seem a bit strange, but using the power of GP we can prove that it is true. Before we proceed, let me make a small note about indices. If a is the base and $b, c, d, \ldots$ are powers of a, the following is true.

$$a^b \times a^c \times a^d = a^{b+c+d}$$

Now, let us get back to our problem and use the above property.

$$3^{1/2} \times 3^{1/4} \times 3^{1/8} \times 3^{1/16} \ldots = 3^{\left(\frac{1}{2}+\frac{1}{4}+\frac{1}{8}+\frac{1}{16}+\ldots\right)}$$

The sum of the series

$$\frac{1}{2}+\frac{1}{4}+\frac{1}{8}+\frac{1}{16}+\ldots = \frac{\frac{1}{2}}{1-\frac{1}{2}} = 1$$

as $a = 1/2, d = 1/2$ and n is infinity.

So $3^{1/2} \times 3^{1/4} \times 3^{1/8} \times 3^{1/16} \ldots$ reduces to 3, as we needed to prove. Try the following problem.

A brain teaser

A climber is 1.6 m tall. Its height increases by 5 cm in the following year. If next year and so on, its height increases by half the amount it increased the previous year, show that it can never become 1.7 m in height.

37

Amazing Inductive Power: Mathematical Induction

This is probably the most simple mathematical technique of all, but truth be told, the results are quite unbelievable when you first come across it. Most of us would wonder at the soundness of the technique and how it can be accepted as geniune. In this chapter I will try and explain a bit more about the technique and then you will be incredulous too.

In drawing scientific conclusions, there are two fundamental processes of reasoning that are commonly employed. One is the process of *deduction*, i.e., the process of reasoning from a general hypothesis or fact to a particular one. The other kind of reasoning is known as *induction* and follows a reverse process.

Induction arrives at a general statement after conclusions derived from particular cases. It begins with observations—we observe and use our intuition to arrive at a tentative conclusion called *conjecture*. In some cases even if we do not have a counter-example, we cannot conclude that a general statement is true simply because it has been found to be true in all the particular cases that have been verified. So how can we prove a general statement, which is true in some particular cases? Such mathematical statements can be proved by using the method known as mathematical induction.

The principle of mathematical induction

Let $P(n)$ be a statement involving the natural number n such that

(i) $P(1)$ is true,

(ii) If $P(k)$ is true, then $P(k+1)$ is also true, where k is a natural number.

Then the statement $P(n)$ is true for every natural number n.

In other words, to prove the statement $P(n)$ to be true for all natural numbers, we need go through only two steps. Firstly, we must verify that $P(1)$ is true. Secondly, we must prove that $P(k+1)$ is true whenever $P(k)$ is true, where k is a natural number.

We now consider some examples.

Can there be an induced formula for the sum of the first n odd natural numbers? Rather, let us try to prove that the sum of the first n odd natural numbers is n^2 using the principle of mathematical induction.

Our $P(n)$ would be

$$P(n) = 1 + 3 + 5 + \ldots (2n - 1) = n^2$$

$2n - 1$ is the nth odd natural number.

For $n = 1, 1 = 1^2$

Therefore, we have completed the first step of the process of mathematical induction.

In the second step, we assume that $P(k)$ is true,

i.e., $P(k) = 1 + 3 + 5 + \ldots + (2k - 1) = k^2$

Now we have to prove that $P(k+1)$ is true whenever $P(k)$ is true.

$$P(k+1) = \underbrace{1 + 3 + 5 + \ldots (2k - 1)}_{P(k)} + [2(k+1) - 1]$$

$$= k^2 + 2k + 2 - 1 = k^2 + 2k + 1 = (k + 1)^2$$

Thus $P(k+1)$ is true whenever $P(k)$ is true. Hence by the principle of mathematical induction, the sum of the first n odd natural numbers is n^2.

Like many of the concepts and methods of mathematics, proof by mathematical induction is not the invention of an individual mathematician. Perhaps the earliest use of the method can be traced back to the Pythagoreans (600 BCE). Traces of mathematical induction are also found in the writings of the Indian mathematician Bhaskaracharya II (1114–1185 CE). But these ancient mathematicians failed to explicitly state the inductive process. This happened centuries later when three mathematicians were credited to have discovered it independently. The Italian mathematician, Francesco Maurolycus used the principle of induction to prove that the sum of the first n odd integers is n^2 in 1575. Though he used it later, Blaise Pascal, the French mathematician, is credited with the origin of the principle of mathematical induction. Later, the Swiss mathematician, James Bernoulli, employed the principle without using the name, to provide a proof of the binomial theorem. The term 'induction' was first used by the English mathematician John Wallis in 1656.

Another example

Let us try to prove that for any natural number n, $n^3 + 2n$ is divisible by 3.

Using the principle of mathematical induction,

For $n = 0, n^3 + 2n = 0 + 0 = 0$, which is divisible for 3.

We then assume that $P(k)$ is true, thus $k^3 + 2k$ is divisible by 3. Now

$$P(k+1) = (k+1)^3 + 2(k+1) = (k^3 + 3k^2 + 3k + 1) + (2k + 2)$$

Manipulating the terms, we have,

$$P(k+1) = (k^3 + 2k) + (3k^2 + 3k + 3)$$
$$= (k^3 + 2k) + 3(k^2 + k + 1)$$

Both the terms are divisible by 3, as $(k^3 + 2k) = P(k)$ is assumed to be divisible by 3 (the induction hypothesis).

Thus for any natural number n, $n^3 + 2n$ is divisible by 3.

38

Strange Geometry: Topology

Draw a circle on a rubber sheet. Now what would happen if you stretch only two sides of the sheet? The circle converts to an ellipse. If the four sides of the sheet are stretched, we could even make a square. Thus all kinds of polygons can be made by manipulating the the corners or sides of the rubber sheet.

Hence we can conclude that a circle, a square, a rectangle, a triangle, and in fact all polygons are topologically equivalent.

Topology comes from the Greek root *topos* (place). Before it was used in mathematics, it was applied to the geographic study of a place in relation to its history. Mathematical topology is an offshoot of the geometry that originated during the 19th century which studied those properties an object retains under deformation—specifically, bending, stretching and squeezing, but not breaking or tearing. *Thus, a triangle is topologically equivalent to a circle but not to a straight line segment.*

Similarly, a solid cube made of modelling clay can be deformed into a ball by kneading. It cannot, however, be moulded into a solid torus (ring) unless a hole is bored through it or two surfaces were joined together. A solid cube is therefore not topologically equivalent to a finger ring.

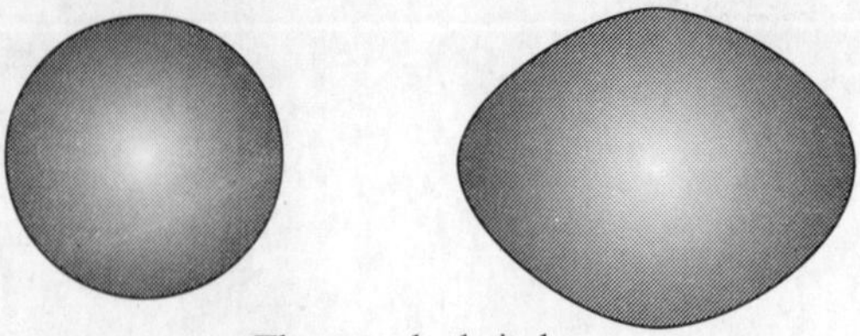

The stretched circle

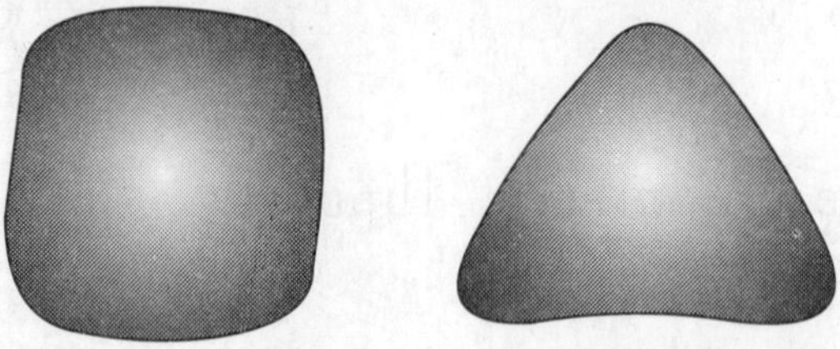

Pulling on the corners

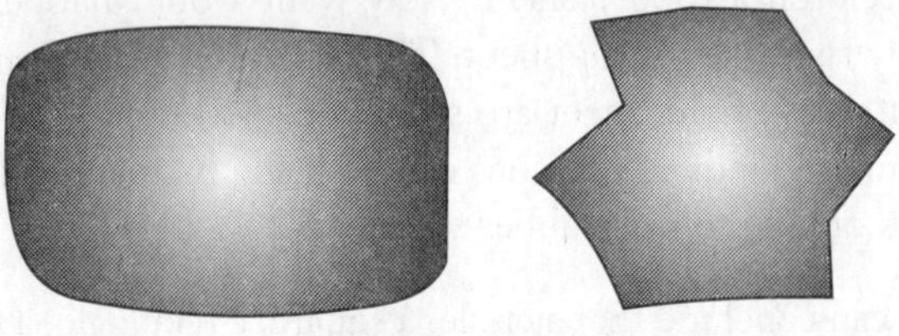

Circle on a rubber sheet

You may be familiar with the famous MÖBIUS strip—a very strange looped strip of paper, which when cut through its centre along the length simply becomes a longer loop rather than getting cut into two parts. Mathematically it is called a single-sided surface.

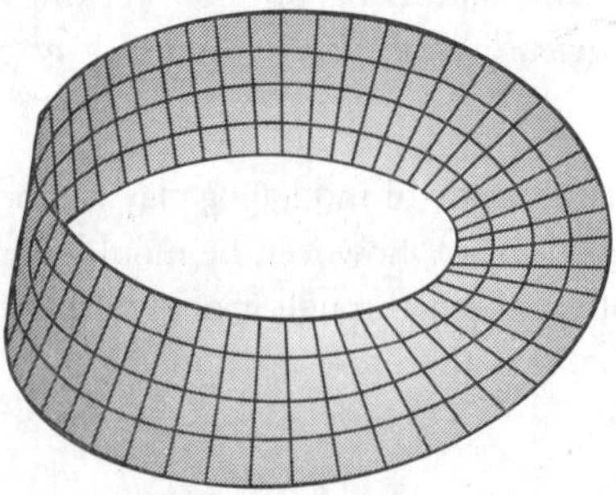

If an ant were to start moving on a Möbius strip from one point on the surface, can you guess where it would reach after completing one round of the strip?

The one-sided nature of a Möbius strip can really be useful in day to day life. Consider the safety belt in a car or any another vehicle—it works on a system of pulleys. The friction on the pulleys can wear down the belt. If the safety belt is given a 180° twist before the ends are sewn, it will last longer, as it will wear equally on both sides, because now the belt has only *one side*.

Topology involves problems concerning deformation of elastic bodies and surfaces. The assumption is that the objects considered are made from a very elastic material. Their shape can be changed at will—they can be bent, distorted, stretched and compressed as much as desired. But you cannot tear them apart or glue parts together.

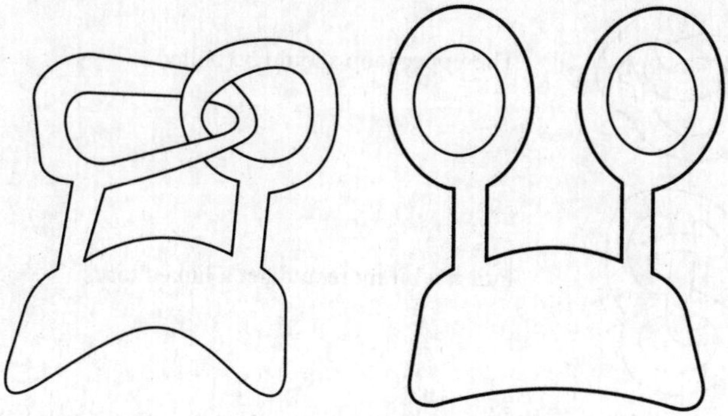

The elastic body on the left can be deformed to make the one shown on the right side or vice versa. That's rubber sheet geometry! Can you try it?

Solution

In this solution, we are moving from the right figure to the one on the left.

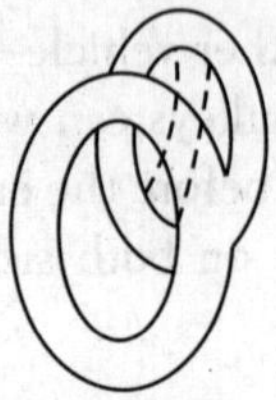

Move one link inside the other

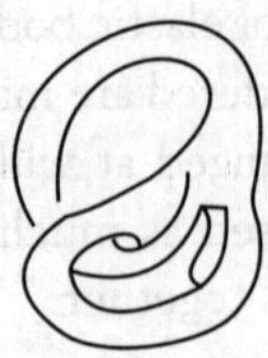

Now move the inner part as depicted to form another loop

The upper loop should be pulled

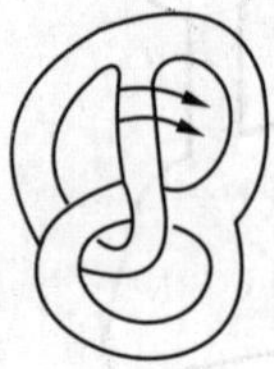

Pull it a bit more and get a linked torus

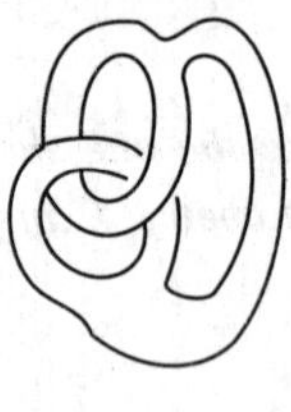

The unlinked torus is converted to a linked torus

39

Redefined Geometry in the Universe

Euclid in his seminal work *Elements* built the foundations of the subject that we are all familiar with and that which we study in our mathematics course—geometry. The subject is also known as Euclidean geometry after its main contributor.

But God had something else in mind which man discovered later and called non-Euclidean geometry.

Where on earth can you find a triangle each of whose interior angles is 90°?

First, think about the question. Our conventional knowledge tells us that the sum of all interior angles of a triangle is 180°. If we had a triangle, all of whose angles were 90°, the sum of all the angles would be 270°—which is impossible.

But take the representation of the earth on a globe with the latitudes and longitudes marked. Consider the lines of longitude which correspond to 0° and 90°; and the equator. These lines intersect in a triangle whose angles are all 90°.

This is the basic tenet of non-Euclidean geometry. On spherical surfaces, the shortest distance between two points is always part of the great circle. In this sense, the great circles play the same role as that of straight lines in a plane. In fact on a sphere, triangles formed from these circles can have the sum of their angles ranging anywhere between 180° and 360°.

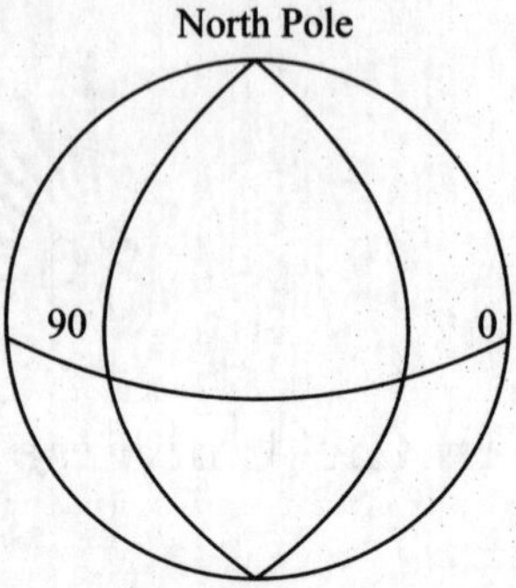

The three angles at North Pole. 0° and 90° longitude add up to more than 180°

Consider the following: Two explorers are 10 km apart when they set off in the same direction and travel at the same speed for two hours. After two hours, they are 22 kms apart! How is this possible? If they start 10 kms apart on different longitudes near the North Pole and walk towards the south, they would soon diverge. There are other ways also.

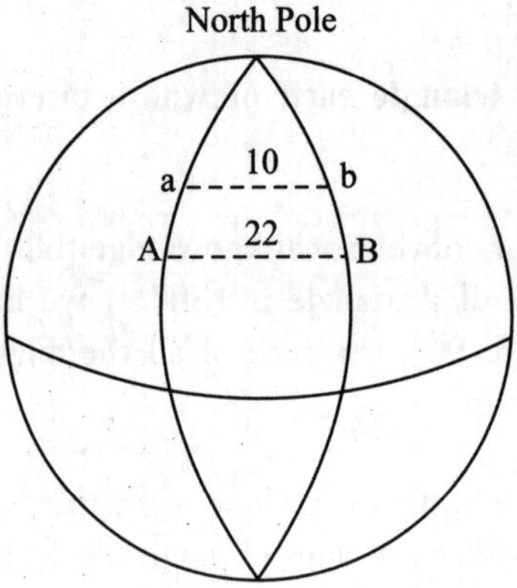

The explorers start from a and b, move towards the equator on different longitudes to reach A and B which are more distant than a and b, as depicted in the figure.

Well, dear reader, this is not all—there is much more seeming impossibilities in non-Euclidean geometry. But it is beyond the scope of this book. I will leave you with the fact that Einstein successfully predicted the deflection of light, which has no mass, in the vicinity of a star or other massive body. This was an extravagant piece of geometrising—the replacement of straight gravitational force by the curvature of a surface. In the theory of relativity, time is considered to be a dimension along with the three dimensions of space. On the closed four-dimensional world thus formed, the history of the universe stands revealed by the tenets of the non-Euclidean universe.

40

Some Dissections

Dissection is perhaps the most recreational aspect of geometry. It has the advantage of being extremely non-equation and non-formula based; using only common sense and plenty of logic. Take a look at a few dissections.

The imperfect chessboard

Dissect the chessboard shown below into two parts so that the parts fit in to make a perfect chessboard.

Pentagon to trapezium

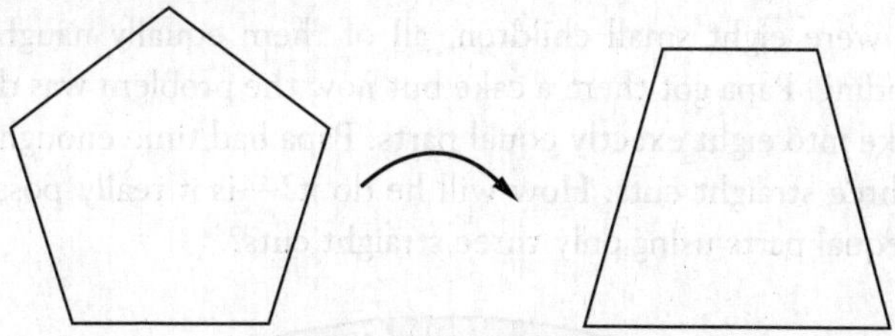

Cut the regular pentagon into four isosceles triangles so that they can be arranged to form a symmetric trapezium.

The next one is different. Think differently—think laterally!

The square problem

There are five identical squares. Make just one straight cut so that they can be rearranged to form a bigger square.

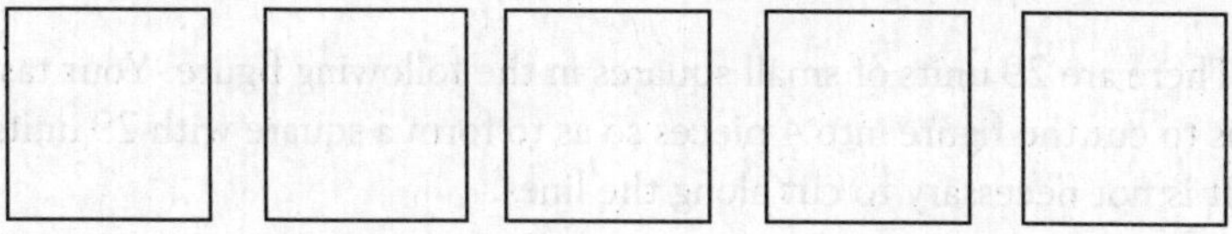

Equilateral dissection

Can you dissect an equilateral triangle into four pieces so that they can be formed into a square? This one is tough.

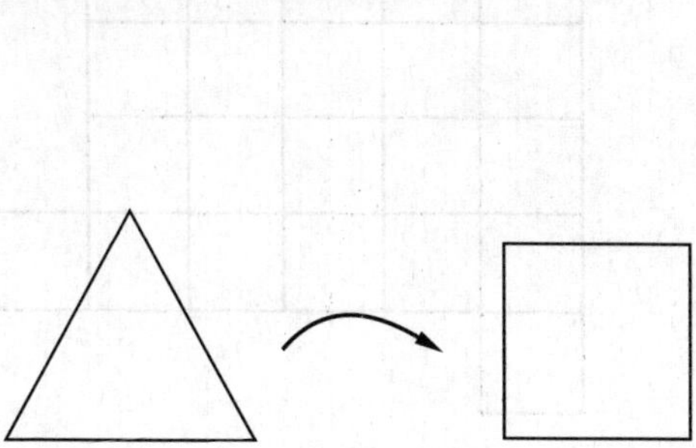

Eight pieces of cake

There were eight small children, all of them equally naughty and demanding. Papa got them a cake but now the problem was dividing the cake into eight exactly equal parts. Papa had time enough to use only three straight cuts. How will he do it?—is it really possible—eight equal parts using only three straight cuts?

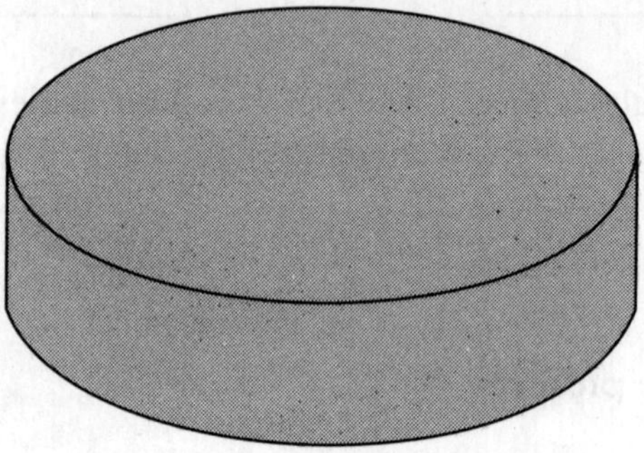

One last problem

There are 29 units of small squares in the following figure. Your task is to cut the figure into 4 pieces so as to form a square with 29 units. It is not necessary to cut along the lines.

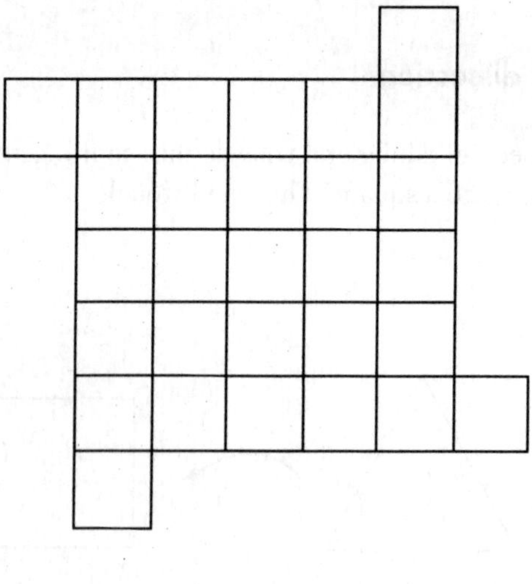

Solutions

The imperfect chessboard

Cut the chessboard as above and rotate the piece by 90°

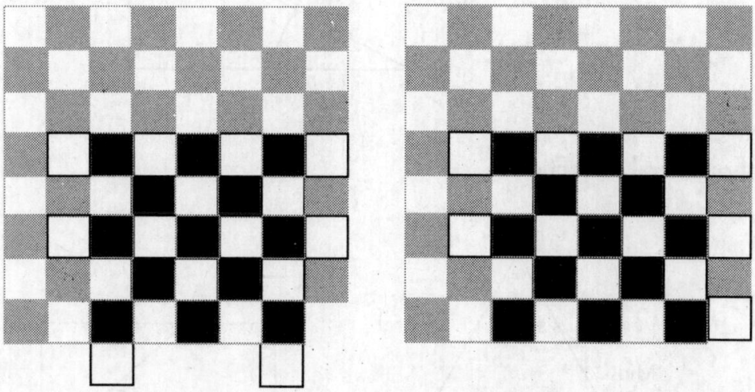

Pentagon to trapezium

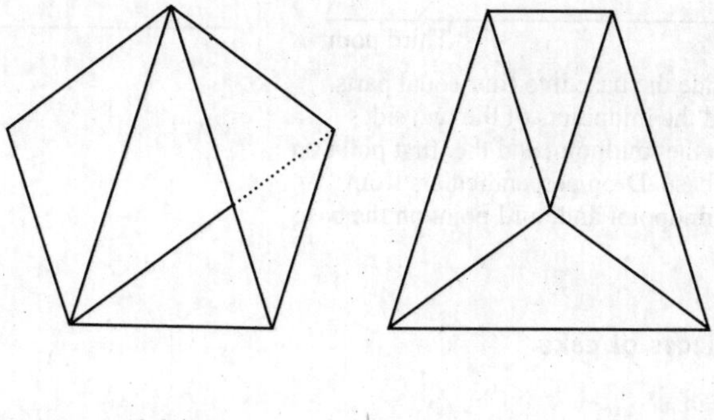

The square problem

This one is really different. Place four of the pieces one upon the other and make a straight cut passing through one corner and centre of the opposite side as shown. Now place the pieces to form a square. Great, isn't it?

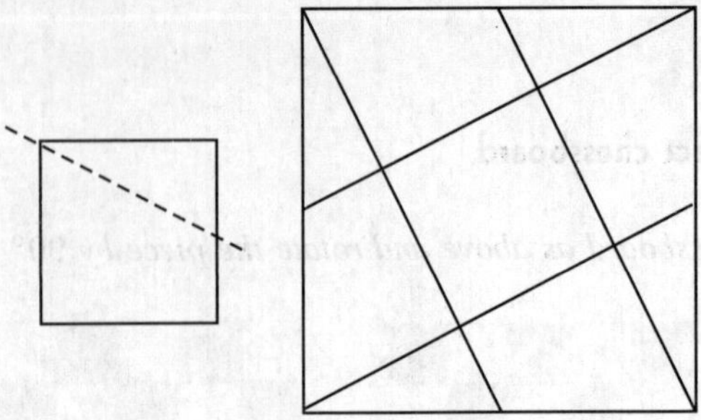

Equilateral dissection

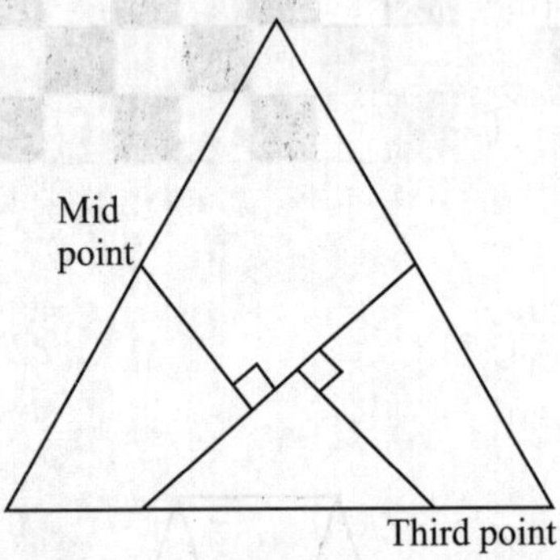

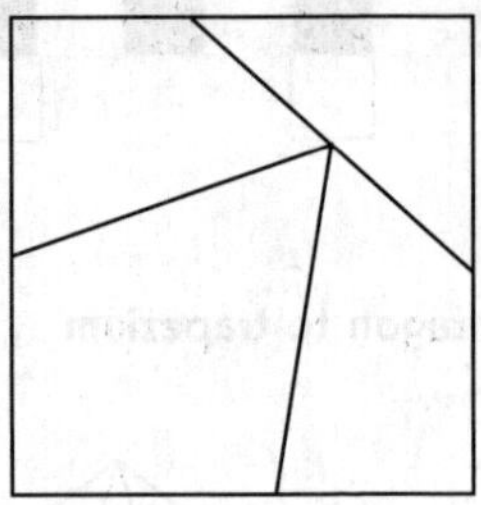

Divide the base into four equal parts.
Find the midpoints of the two sides
Join the midpoint and the first point on the base. Drop perpendiculars from the midpoint and third point on the base

Eight pieces of cake

Papa has to first make two cuts on top of the cake in the shape of a cross. The third cut has to be through the middle of the cake, and we have our eight equal pieces. See the advantage of thinking laterally!

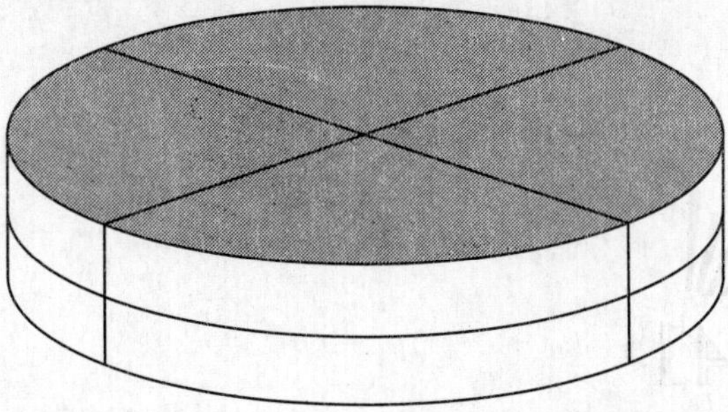

One last problem

Cut along the lines shown and arrange to form a square with $\sqrt{29}$ units as one side.

41

Why Worry About Population Explosion?

Many of us are concerned about living space, resources for the next generation, environment etc., all on account of the growing population. 'The world is not big enough to accommodate so many people', is an oft quoted remark. But is there really cause for alarm?

Many doomsday prophets proclaim that by a certain year there would be no food or space for human beings. We might have to consider living on some other planet or in buildings made in space. I tried to figure out, using a small calculation, how much space is really required. If all the people in the world were told to stand side by side, giving them enough space to stand freely, how much space would they occupy?

If we assume each person to be of normal height and weight, a square of say *2 feet by 2 feet* would be sufficient for one person.

Considering the population of the world to be about 6,000,000,000 i.e., 6 billion or 600 crore (it is now closer to 700 crore), the space required would be

$$(6 \times 10^9) \times (2 \times 2) \text{ sq feet area}$$

What does this amount to? If we consider this space to be a square, the length of one side of the square would be

$$\sqrt{\{(6 \times 10^9) \times (2 \times 2)\}}$$

which is just about 155000 feet.

If we are to consider this in the metric system, 1 km is about 3300 feet. So the square size would be just 47 kilometres!

I wonder then what is the problem?—the whole world can be fit in Delhi itself, with some adjoining areas of Gurgaon. Just think about it—*a city 47 km wide and 47 km long can accommodate the whole world*!

Of course, here we are not considering the basic human need for personal space and land for cultivation. Besides which, we are just proving that, mathematically, it is possible.

Okay, what about India? How big a city would be required to pack all the Indians together?

There are about 100 crore of us.

If we follow the same lines as we did for the population of the world, we would need a square of side

$$\sqrt{(1 \times 10^9) \times (2 \times 2)},$$

which is about 63000 feet, just about 19 km × 19 km. So towns of the size of Ahmedabad or Lucknow are big enough for all Indians to be packed together.

Another interesting question: How much human blood is there in the Universe (this, of course is being very human-centric, there are infinitely more non-humans, maybe even non-earthlings, than humans in the Universe)? If we are to have a container to store all this blood, how big should the container be?

An average human being has about 4 litres of blood, and there are about 6 billion people on the earth. Therefore, the total amount of blood in the Universe is

$$6,000,000,000 = 2.4 \times 10^{10} \text{ litres}$$

Now $1 m^3 = 1000$ litres

Thus we would require a cube with volume $2.4 \times 10^7 m^3$

This means that the side of the cube will be about 290 m, which is alright for the length and breadth but a little too much for the height.

If we consider turning the racecourse at Delhi into a container for all the blood, with an area of about 2 sq km, we would only need a depth of 12 m. Interesting!

Calculation has revealed that the speed of growth of human hair is about 10^{-8} km per hour. Quick, isn't it?

Try calculating the speed of your growth from less than 18 inches to whatever your height is now!

42

Nature's Own Series: Fibonacci

In 1202 the mathematician, Leonardo of Pisa, also called Fibonacci, published an influential treatise, *Liber Abaci*. It contained the following recreational problem: How many pairs of rabbits can be produced from a single pair in one year, if it is assumed that every month, each pair begets a new pair which from the second month becomes productive?

Assuming that in the first month there is just one newly-born pair,

- new-born pairs become fertile from their second month on,
- each month, every fertile pair begets a new pair, and
- the rabbits never die,

straightforward calculation generates the sequence shown in Figure 42.1.

The bee ancestry code

Fibonacci described the sequence 'encoded in the ancestry of a male bee'. One can derive this series by using the following facts:

- If an egg is laid by a single female, it hatches a male.
- If, however, the egg is fertilised by a male, it hatches a female.
- Thus, a male bee will always have one parent, and a female bee will have two. If one traces the ancestry of this male bee (1

bee), he has 1 female parent A (a total of 1 bee at this level). A had 2 parents, a male and a female B (a total of 2 bees at this level). B had two parents, a male and a female C, and the male had one female D (a total of 3 bees). C and D each had two parents, and the male had one (a total of 5 bees). This will be clear from Figure 42.2.

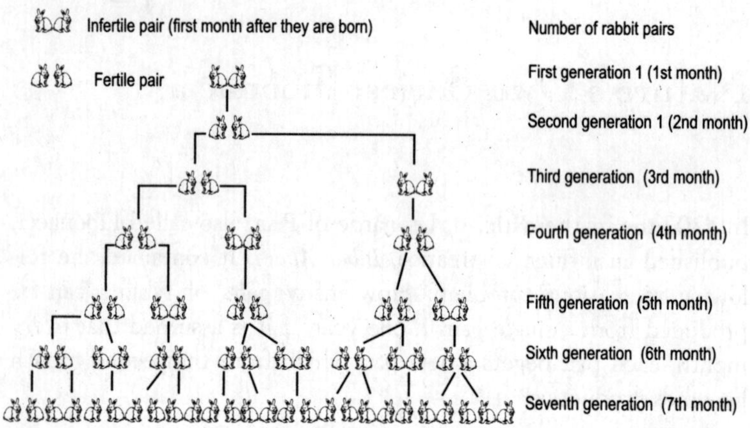

Figure 42.1 *Multiplication of rabbits*

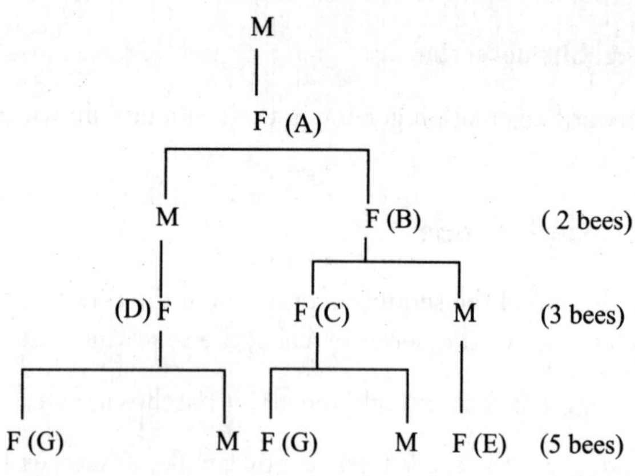

Figure 42.2 *Ancestry of bees*

If one continues this series, we get a perfectly accurate depiction of the sequence now known as the Fibonacci sequence.

The above numbers (1, 1, 2, 3, 5) represent the first terms of the Fibonacci sequence in which each term (except the first two) is found by adding the two terms immediately preceeding it; in general,

$$F_n = F_{n-1} + F_{n-2},$$

a relation that was not recognised until about 1600.

The most astonishing replication of this series in nature is in *phyllotaxis*. Phyllotaxis is the distribution or arrangement of leaves on a stem. In fact, this term means more than just the distribution of leaves; it extends to petals, seeds, florets, and branches. If we look at a plant from above, we will notice that the leaves are not arranged directly above one another, but in a way that optimises their exposure to the sun and rain. The Fibonacci numbers occur when counting both the number of times we go around the stem until we encounter one directly above the starting one and when counting the number of leaves we meet on the way.

Let us consider just one leaf on the bottom of a stem—call it leaf 0 (as in Figure 42.3). If we count the leaves up the stem until we come to one which is directly above the starting one, we get 8, which is a term of the Fibonacci sequence. Again, if we count the number of times we revolve about the stem to reach this leaf, we get 5. This number, too, is a term of the sequence. In fact 5 and 8 are consecutive Fibonacci numbers, the ratio of which is 1.6.

Thus we can see that phyllotaxis are very closely related to the Fibonacci series and what is called the *golden ratio* φ—1.6180339— which is another of Nature's great numbers (it will be discussed in more detail in the next chapter).

The interesting thing is that the convergence of the ratio of successive terms to φ is very rapid,

$$\frac{F_n}{\lim x \to \infty \; F_{n-1}} = \varphi(1.6180339\ldots),$$

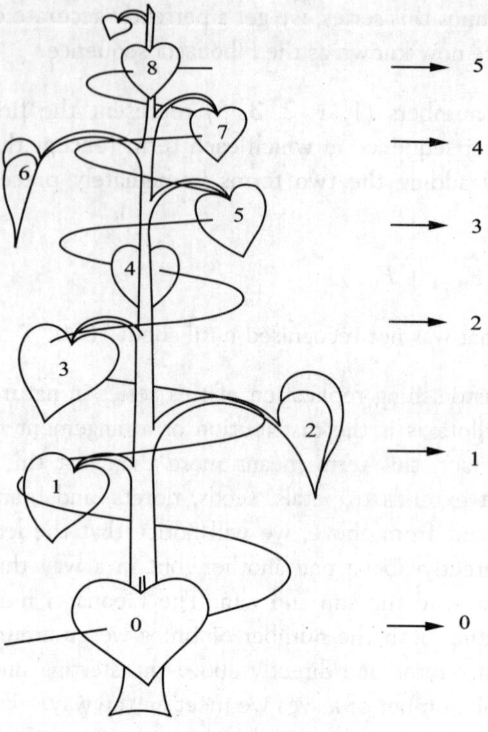

Figure 42.3 *Phyllotaxis*

where F_n is the nth term in the Fibonacci series.

Golden ratio = **1.61803398874989484820**4586834365 ...

From the table given below it can be seen that as the series grows, the ratio of successive terms converges to the golden mean.

Ratio	Value	Correct up to
F_3/F_2	2	0 places
F_5/F_4	1.5	0 places
F_7/F_6	**1.6**25	1 place
F_{13}/F_{12}	**1.6180**555556	4 places
F_{16}/F_{15}	**1.61803**27869	5 places
F_{22}/F_{21}	**1.61803**71353	5 places
F_{49}/F_{48}	**1.6180339887498948482**2393	19 places
F_{50}/F_{49}	**1.618033988749894848**19719	18 places

Lilies have 3 petals, buttercups 5, delphiniums 8, marigold 13, asters 21 and daisies 34, 55 and sometimes 89. The principle that plants follow is to use space so as to receive optimum amount of sunlight and optimally interact with the environment.

Consider a branch growing on a tree. As the branch grows outwards, the leaves are generated at regular angular intervals. But these intervals are not exact rational multiples of 360°. If we examine the growth of leaves on various trees, we will see that the leaves are generated (*approximately*) after

2/5 of a revolution of a circle for oak, cherry, apple, plum,

1/2 for some grasses, lime, linden,

1/3 for beech, hazel,

3/8 for rose, polar, willow and

5/13 for almond.

All these approximations are called phyllotactic ratios and you will notice that the *numerator and denominator are Fibonacci numbers*.

The arrangement of seeds on a sunflower is perhaps the most illustrative example of the Fibonacci series in Nature. The seeds are arranged in two families of spirals—34 winding clockwise (Figure 42.4) and 55 anti-clockwise; or 55 and 89 in the same order. In larger sunflowers, the number of spirals may even be 89, 144. The same pattern is observed in daisies. Why this happens is for the botanist to find out. All we can deduce is that this may be the optimal way to receive maximum sunlight.

Many of Nature's patterns are related to the golden ratio and the Fibonacci numbers. For instance, consider the type of spirals found in unicellular foraminifera, sunflowers, seashells, animal horns and tusks, beaks and claws, whirlpools, hurricanes, and spiral galaxies. All these spirals are logarithmic or equiangular spirals—an equiangular spiral does not alter its shape as its size increases. Because of this remarkable property (known as self-similarity), it was known in earlier times as the miraculous spiral. And if you look further, you will notice that the spiral gets wider (or further from its origin) by a factor of the golden ratio for every quarter turn it makes. These spirals are also known as golden spirals.

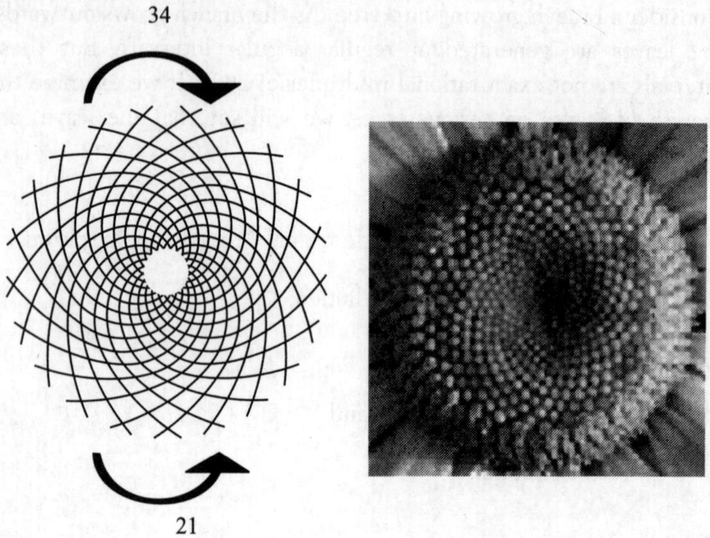

Figure 42.4 *The florets in the head of a sunflower form two intersecting sets of spirals—one winding clockwise with 34 seeds, the other anti-clockwise with 21 seeds.*

The appearance of the Fibonacci sequence in Nature seems to be a by-product of a physical process. The plant or living organism responds to physical constraints and not really to a mathematical rule.

Here is something arithmetically interesting about this sequence,

$$1^2 + 1^2 = 1 \times 2$$

$$1^2 + 1^2 + 2^2 = 2 \times 3$$

$$1^2 + 1^2 + 2^2 + 3^2 = 3 \times 5$$

$$1^2 + 1^2 + 2^2 + 3^2 + 5^2 = 5 \times 8$$

$$1^2 + 1^2 + 2^2 + 3^2 + 5^2 + 8^2 = 8 \times 13$$

Can you see the pattern?

The sum of the squares of the Fibonacci terms is equal to the product of the last term and the term next in the series.

i.e., $1^2 + 1^2 + 2^2 + 3^2 + 5^2 + \ldots\ldots + F_n^2 = F_n \times F_{n+1}$

Another interesting formula given by Edouard Lucas (1842–1891), a French mathematician, is

$$F_n^2 + F_{n+1}^2 = F_{2n+1}$$

Let us consider an example. $F_4 = 3, F_5 = 5$, thus $3^2 + 5^2 = 34$, which is the 9th Fibonacci number $(2 \times 4 + 1)$.

Lucas was the one who gave the series of numbers 0, 1, 1, 2, 3, 5, 8, 13, ... the name, *Fibonacci numbers*. While investigating Fibonacci number patterns, he also discovered the occurrence of a similar series

2, 1, 3, 4, 7, 11, 18, ...

Here we start from 2 and 1 (in this order) instead of 0 and 1 for the (ordinary) Fibonacci numbers, but the rule is the same. There is an interesting relationship between the Lucas series and the Fibonacci series.

n	**0**	**1**	**2**	**3**	**4**	**5**	**6**	**7**	**8**	**9**	**10**
F_n	0	1	1	2	3	5	8	13	21	34	55
L_n	2	1	3	4	7	11	18	29	47	76	123

1. $5F(n) = L(n-1) + L(n+1)$ for all integers n

2. $L(n) = F(n-1) + F(n+1)$ for all integers n

Another interesting thing about the Lucas number is

$$F_{2n} = F_n \times L_n$$

There is a formula known as the Binet's formula for calculating the nth Fibonacci number,

$$F_n = \frac{(1+\sqrt{5})^n - (1-\sqrt{5})^n}{2^n\sqrt{5}}$$

Let me leave you with one more interesting thing about such sequences—the convergence of the ratio of successive terms to the golden mean holds true for any two disparate starting numbers.

43

Nature's Own Number: φ (Phi)

Aesthetic judgments are ephemeral—what is beautiful now, ten years down the line may be considered ugly. These judgments may also be developed within the culture of a mathematical age and culture, and their validity is similar to that of a school or period of art. It was once maintained that the most beautiful rectangle has sides whose ratio is equal to the *golden ratio*.

Nowadays, we derive aesthetic delight from the golden ratio, φ (Greek alphabet 'phi') not for itself *per se* but because of the diverse and unexpected places in which it arises.

One such diverse place is the geometry of the regular pentagon (Figure 43.1).

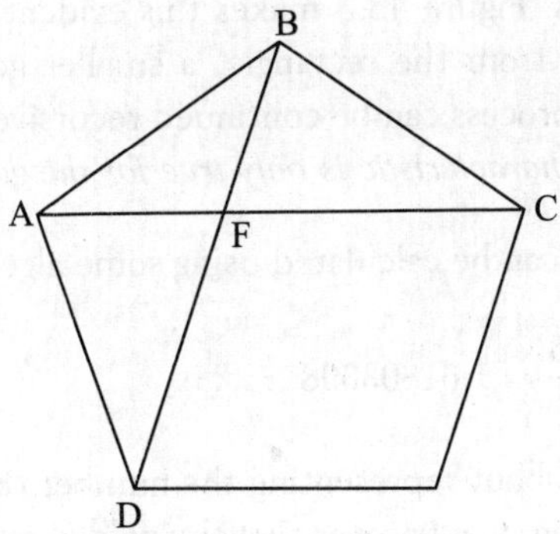

Figure 43.1 *Regular pentagon*

The diagonal AC divides the diagonal BD in the golden ratio, φ. The importance of this ratio is that if F is the intersection of the two diagonals then,

$$\frac{\mathrm{BF}}{\mathrm{FD}} = \frac{\mathrm{FD}}{\mathrm{BD}}$$

The golden ratio (Figure 43.2) is thought of as the divine ratio. It is the most perfect way to divide a rectangle.

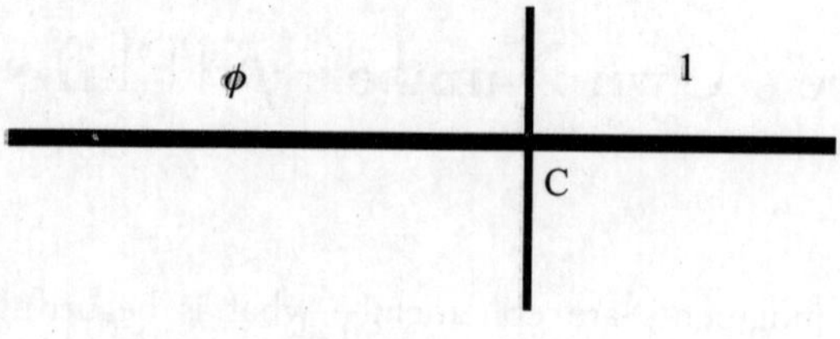

Figure 43.2 *The golden ratio*

$$\varphi : 1 = (\varphi + 1) : \varphi$$

The line segment is divided at C so that the ratio of the larger part to the smaller part is the same as the whole to the larger part. The Greeks called it the method of dividing a line into the 'extreme and mean ratio'.

Rectangles whose sides are in the golden ratio are called golden rectangles. Interestingly, if we draw a golden rectangle (GR), this golden rectangle can be formed out of a nested set of ever decreasing golden rectangles. Figure 43.3 makes this evident. By cutting out a square of unit 1 from the rectangle, a smaller golden rectangle is formed and the process can be continued recursively. *It is important to note that this characteristic is only true for the golden rectangle.*

The golden ratio can be calculated using some algebra.

$$\varphi = \frac{1 + \sqrt{5}}{2} = 1.61803398\ldots\ldots$$

What is exciting about representing the number this way, is that by some manipulation, we discover that the golden ratio is equal to one plus its reciprocal.

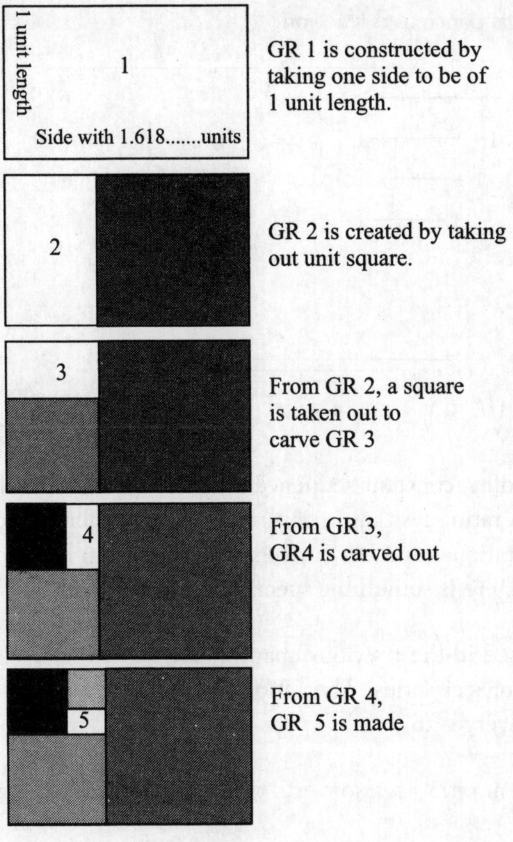

Figure 43.3 *Nested golden rectangles: This process is also reversible. Starting with a GR if we add a square of longer side, we will get another GR and so on. This property is experienced only with GR*

$$\varphi = 1 + \frac{1}{\varphi}$$

But what really is so special about this number, that it has been revered by humanity for ages? It is believed (not really very scientifically) that God created everything with this ratio in mind. You may read Dan Brown's famous *The Da Vinci Code* for more on this. All the artists of the Renaissance period used this ratio for their art forms like the canvas ratio, human figures etc.

Look at this continued fraction,

$$\varphi = 1 + \cfrac{1}{1 + \cfrac{1}{1 + \cfrac{1}{1 + \cfrac{1}{1 + \cdots}}}}$$

Also,

$$\varphi = \sqrt{1 + \sqrt{1 + \sqrt{1 + \sqrt{1 + \ldots\ldots}}}}$$

This unending, constant sequence of 1s in the continued fraction for the golden ratio says that, measured in terms of continued fractions, it is the irrational number furthest removed from being rational. So certainly there is something special about this ratio.

As discussed in the previous chapter, the golden ratio also pops up in the Fibonacci series. The ratio of successive terms of this series finally converges to φ.

The golden ratio is also very typically related to trigonometric functions,

$$\varphi = 1 + 2\sin(\pi/10) = 1 + 2\sin 18^\circ$$

$$\varphi = 2\cos(\pi/5) = 2\cos 36^\circ$$

The golden section of the circumference of a circle leads to the golden angle of 137.51°. This angle (Figure 43.4) is important in phyllotaxis (the arrangement of leaves on the stem of a plant). Plants utilise this angle to get minimum superposition and maximum sun exposure to the assimilating members.

The nth Fibonacci number can also be found by the expression,

$$F(n) = \frac{\varphi^n - (1-\varphi)^n}{\sqrt{5}}$$

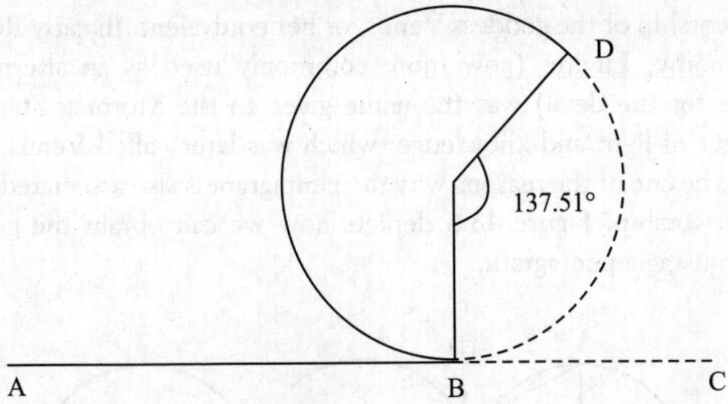

Figure 43.4 *AC is the circumference of the circle flattened out from D. B divides AC such that AB:BC = φ: 1,if the angle subtended is 137.51°. Thus 137.51° is called the golden angle.*

The Fibonacci recurrence is also observed in successive powers of φ.

This actually means that

$$\varphi^{n+1} = \varphi^n + \varphi$$

Construction of golden mean

One way of constructing the golden mean, of course, is through a pentagon or pentagram which will be explained in a little while. But another very nice method has been discovered.

Construct 3 circles of 1 unit diameter, all the centres in a line. Join the top-most point of the first circle to the bottom-most point of the third circle (as depicted in Figure 43.5).

Using the Pythagoras theorem, we find that the line BC is $\sqrt{5}$.

$$\text{BE} + \text{CD} = \sqrt{5} - 1 \text{ and BE} = \text{CD},$$

Thus $\text{CD} = (\sqrt{5} - 1)/2 = 1/\varphi,$

and $\text{CE} = 1 + \text{CD} = (\sqrt{5} + 1)/2 = \varphi$

The pentagram has long been associated with the planet Venus, and the worship of the goddess Venus, or her equivalent. In early Roman astronomy, Lucifer (now more commonly used as an alternative name for the devil) was the name given to the Morning Star, the bringer of light and knowledge, which was later called Venus. This could be one of the reasons why the pentagram is also associated with devil worship. Figure 43.6 depicts how we can obtain the golden mean using a pentagram.

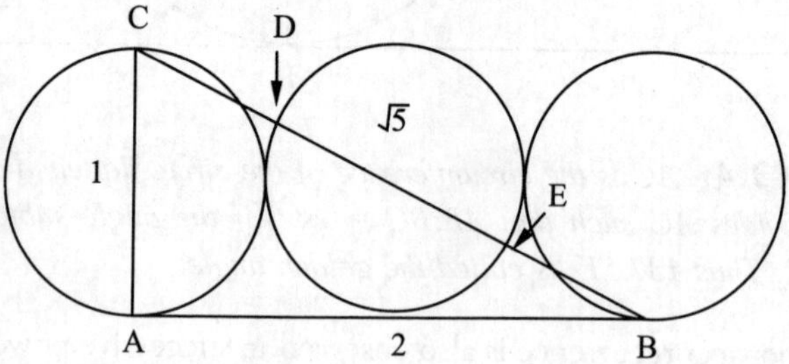

Figure 43.5 *Construction of golden mean*

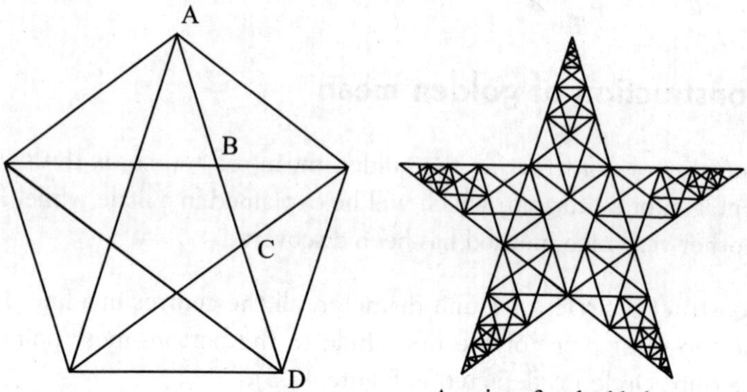

The pentagram is formed by joining the vertices of the pentagon. The special property of the pentagram is that each line can divided into several smaller segments, and if you divide the length of the longer segment with the shorter segment of any pair of segments, you will get the golden ratio

A series of embedded pentagrams can be constructed to form a larger pentagram, which is shown above

$$\frac{AD}{AC} = \frac{AC}{CD} = \frac{CD}{BC}$$

Figure 43.6 *Construction of golden mean using a pentagram*

44

The Story of e and π

Pi goes on and on and on ...
And e is just as cursed.
I wonder: Which is larger
When their digits are reversed?

Anonymous

There are two friends in the city of mathematics, named e and π (the Greek letter *pi*). They have an interesting story to tell, and a very strange relationship with a very imaginary citizen called i, who is the square root of -1. Father Euler got them together in such a way that none could understand the relationship,

$$e^{i\pi} + 1 = 0$$

Richard Feynman, the great American physicist and Noble Laureate called Euler's formula (from which the identity is derived) '*the most remarkable formula in mathematics*'. Feynman, as well as many others, found this formula remarkable because it links some very fundamental mathematical constants.

Leonhard Euler (1707–1783), one of the founders of pure mathematics was born in Basel, Switzerland. He introduced many current notations, such as $\sum$ for summation; $\int n$ for the sum of divisors of n; the symbol e for the base of natural logarithms; a, b, and c for the sides of a triangle and A, B, and C for the opposite angles; the letter 'f' and parentheses for a function; the use of the symbol π for the ratio of the circumference to the diameter in a circle; and i for $\sqrt{(-1)}$. Thus in his honour, the natural logarithm 2.718 . . . was designated as e.

Most of us know π—π is the ratio of the circumference of a circle to its diameter. We may even have heard of the natural logarithm e, and wondered why anyone would have chosen such a strange number for logarithms when base 10 could have worked just as well. Even the square root of $-1, i$ is an impossible kind of number. But it was invented by Euler to solve some very complex, generally incomprehensible equations—we will discuss these in the next chapter.

Let us start with π. Its value is 22/7 or 3.14 as is commonly known. The history of the calculation of the value of π is quite exciting.

Archimedes calculated that π lies between $3\frac{10}{71}$ and $3\frac{10}{70}$ (22/7). Later, around 500 CE, Chinese scholars showed that π is between 3.14152927 and 3.1415926. In 1596 Ludolph van Ceulen (1540–1610) of Cologne used the method of comparing a circle to the straight-sided figure that is approximately a circle, a regular polygon with many sides, to calculate π to 32 places. His result was engraved on his tombstone and to this day the Germans call π, the *Ludolphine number*.

In the 17th century, John Wallis (1616–1703) discovered

$$\frac{\pi}{2} = \frac{2}{1} \times \frac{2}{3} \times \frac{4}{3} \times \frac{4}{5} \times \frac{6}{5} \times \frac{6}{7} \times \cdots$$

in which the numerators are the even numbers from 2 given twice, while the denominators are odd numbers in a similar pattern. James Gregory and Wilhelm Gottfried Leibniz discovered an even simpler pattern for an infinite sum:

$$\frac{\pi}{4} = \frac{1}{1} - \frac{1}{3} + \frac{1}{5} - \frac{1}{7} + \frac{1}{9} - \frac{1}{11} + \cdots.$$

In the 18th century, Johann Lambert solved one of the problems connected with π. He showed that π is irrational; in other words, it cannot be expressed as a finite decimal, nor can it have a simple repeating pattern as a decimal.

Knowing that it cannot be expressed finitely has not deterred number enthusiasts. There are scores of computers and mathematicians calculating the value of π, and there is stiff competition to find the value of π up to the largest decimal place. In 2002, Yasumasa Kanada and fellow researchers at Japan's Information Technology Center set a new record for finding the number of digits of π, a whopping 1.24 trillion decimal places. This calculation took about *six hundred hours*. This fascination for calculating the value of π can even be seen in television shows. In the *Star Trek*[2] episode 'Wolf in the Fold', when Enterprise's computer is taken over by an evil consciousness, Spock tells the computer to compute π to the last digit. This renders the entity incapacitated as all its resources are dedicated to this impossible task.

π can be expressed as a continued fraction,

$$\frac{4}{\pi} = 1 + \cfrac{1}{3 + \cfrac{4}{5 + \cfrac{9}{7 + \cfrac{16}{9 + \cfrac{25}{11 + \cfrac{36}{13 + \cdots}}}}}}$$

Notice the odd numbers and squares. Amazing!

π is a beautiful number and can be expressed in various interesting series.

$$\frac{\pi}{2} = 1 + \frac{1}{3} + \frac{1.2}{3.5} + \frac{1.2.3}{3.5.7} + \ldots \text{ by Euler}$$

$$\frac{\pi^2}{6} = 1 + \frac{1}{2^2} + \frac{1}{3^2} + \frac{1}{4^2} + \ldots$$

[2] A poular science fiction television series set in the distant future and depicting the adventures of a group of humans and aliens travelling in a spaceship called the *Enterprise*. Spock is the scientific officer of the ship.

$$\frac{\pi^4}{90} = 1 + \frac{1}{2^4} + \frac{1}{3^4} + \frac{1}{4^4} + \dots$$

Using only odd numbers,

$$\frac{\pi^2}{8} = 1 + \frac{1}{3^2} + \frac{1}{5^2} + \frac{1}{7^2} + \dots$$

Euler's number, e, came to the notice of many mathematicians at about the same time, in the early 18th century. It appeared as a result of several different lines of investigation and became known as a *natural number*. You may wonder why.

The number e has a physical meaning. It occurs naturally in any situation where a quantity increases at a rate proportional to its value (such a growth is called an *exponential growth*), such as a bank account producing interest, or a population increasing as its members reproduce. The number e is the factor by which a bank account earning compounding interest continually (or a reproducing population whose offspring are also capable of reproduction, or any similar quantity that grows at a rate proportional to its current value) will increase, if without the compounding (or without the offspring being capable of further reproduction), it would have doubled.

Obviously, the quantity will increase more if the increase is based on the total current quantity (including previous increases), than if it is only based on the original quantity (with previous increases not counted). How much more? The number e answers this question. To put it in another way, the number e is related to how much more money you will earn under compound interest than you would under simple interest.

QUESTION *If you would earn 100% interest (i.e., your money would double) under simple interest, how much money would you end up with under compound interest?*

ANSWER *You would have e times your original amount.*

REASONING e can be expressed as the following series.

$$e = 1 + 1 + \frac{1}{2!} + \frac{1}{3!} + \frac{1}{4!} + \dots$$

and therefore if x be any number,

$$e^x = \left(1 + \frac{1}{n}\right)^{nx}, \text{ when } n \text{ tends to infinity.}$$

Now, if we come to our problem, the principal is the amount of money we started with. The process by which its interest is added to the principal at regular periods of time is called compounding of interest. The amount earned increases by jumps at these interest periods in the following manner. If r is the rate of interest and the interest accrued is added to the principal at the end of each year, then after x years, the accumulated amount of an original principal of say Rs 1 will be

$$(1 + r)^x.$$

If the principal had the interest added to it, not at the end of each year, but at the end of each pth part of a year, then after x years, the principal would amount to

$$\left(1 + \frac{r}{p}\right)^{xp}.$$

To simplify the formula, let us consider this only for 1 year i.e., $x = 1$. Calculated this way, the principal of Rs 1 amounts after one year to

$$\left(1 + \frac{r}{p}\right)^{p}. \text{ Let } p/r = n, \text{ thus we have } \left(1 + \frac{1}{n}\right)^{nr}.$$

If we now let the interest be calculated at shorter and shorter intervals, i.e., *p tends to infinity* or *n tends to infinity*, the limiting case will signify in a sense that the interest is compounded continuously, at each instant. And we see that the total amount after one year will be e^r times the original principal (remember the formula for e given before). Similarly, if the interest is calculated in this manner, an original principal of Rs 1 will have grown after x years to an amount e^{rx}, where x may be any number, integral or otherwise.

Now the reader can appreciate why this strange number $e =$ 2.71828182845904523536028747135266249775 is used as the natural logarithm—it is the only logarithm base which has a rate of change the same as the quantity which is changing.

e, can also be expressed as a continued fraction,

$$e = 2 + \cfrac{1}{1 + \cfrac{1}{2 + \cfrac{2}{3 + \cfrac{3}{4 + \cfrac{4}{5 + \cfrac{5}{6 + \cdots}}}}}}$$

One more fact: the differential of e^x is e^x itself! It is the only function that remains unaltered when differentiated.

45

i, Is it Really Imaginary?

Despite their name, imaginary numbers are just as 'real' as real numbers. One way to understand this is by realising that numbers themselves are abstractions, and the abstractions can be valid even when they are not recognised in a given context. For example, fractions such as 3/4 and 5/7 are meaningless to a person counting eggs, but essential to a person comparing the sizes of different stones. Similarly, negative numbers such as -3 and -5 are meaningless when keeping score in a cricket match, but essential when keeping track of debits and credits in a bank account.

Imaginary numbers follow a similar pattern. For most real tasks, real numbers (or even rational numbers) offer an adequate description of data, and imaginary numbers have no meaning; however, in many areas of science and mathematics, imaginary numbers (and complex numbers in general) are essential for describing reality. Imaginary numbers have essential concrete applications in a variety of sciences and related areas such as signal processing, control theory, electromagnetism, quantum mechanics, and cartography.

For example, in electrical engineering, when analysing AC circuitry, the values for the electrical voltage (and current) are expressed as imaginary or complex numbers known as phasors. These are real voltages that can cause damage/harm to either humans or equipment even if their values contain no 'real part'.

Euler's formula, which states that, for any real number x,

$$e^{ix} = \cos x + i \sin x$$

is widely used to express signals (e.g., electromagnetic) that vary periodically over time as a combination of sine and cosine functions.

An important mathematical warning

The imaginary unit is written as in all mathematics contexts, but great care needs to be taken when formulae involves radicals. Quite simply, it can easily be proven that $1 = -1$ (mathematically impossible). Observe,

$$-1 = i.i$$

$$i.i = \sqrt{-1}.\sqrt{-1} = \sqrt{-1.-1} = \sqrt{1} = 1$$

You might ask, 'what is wrong with this?'. Well, the calculation rule is only valid for real, non-negative values of a and b. The word *imaginary* was first applied to the square root of a negative number by Rene Descartes around 1635. Descartes wrote that although one can imagine that every Nth degree equation had N roots, there were no real numbers for some of these imagined roots. Around 1685, the English mathematician, John Wallis wrote, 'we have before had occasion to make mention of negative squares, and imaginary roots'. Some mathematicians have suggested that the name be changed to avoid the stigma it seems to create in young students; 'Why do we have to learn them if they aren't even real?' Before this misguiding word 'imaginary', the square roots of negatives were called *sophisticated or subtle*.

The letter i for the imaginary unit was first used by Leonhard Euler (1707–1783) in a memoir presented in 1777 but not published until 1794 in his *Institutionum Calculi Integralis*.

46

The Eternal Search for Primes

All over the world, for centuries together, amateurs, serious mathematicians have all been involved in finding primes. Will the search ever end? Unfortunately, or fortunately, depending on whose side you are on, it has been declared that there are infinite primes. With this declaration, the hope is still alive that anyone, be he a great mathematician or just an amateur enthusiast, can discover a new prime. But there is stiff competition. The internet has a site belonging to GIMPS, *Great Internet Mersenne Prime Search*, which is dedicated to the search of prime numbers. Computers are getting faster and more efficient, thus assisting the prime algorithm in searching, verifying and authenticating the *primality* of a number. which is dedicated to the search of prime numbers. Computers are getting faster and more efficient, thus assisting the prime algorithm in searching, verifying and authenticating the *primality* of a number.

On September 4, 2006, Dr. Curtis Cooper and Dr. Steven Boone of Central Missouri State University and members of GIMPS discovered the *44th known Mersenne prime*, $2^{32,582,657} - 1$. The new prime at 9,808,358 digits is 650,000 digits larger than their previous record prime found in December 2005, $2^{30,402,457} - 1$ (this number is 9,152,052 digits long); it was the 43rd *known Mersenne prime*.

The next largest known prime is $2^{25964951} - 1$ (this number is 7,816,230 digits long); it is the 42nd known *Mersenne prime*.

M25964951 was found on February 18, 2005 by Martin Nowak (also a member of GIMPS).

The reader must be wondering about the designation Mersenne—but then what is a prime number and why is it so important?

A *prime number* is a natural number greater than 1 that can be divided without any remainder only by 1 and itself. Thus the first few prime numbers are

$$2, 3, 5, 7, 11, 13, 17, 19, 23, 29, \ldots$$

A prime number of the form $2^n - 1$ (i.e., one unit less than a power of 2) is known as a *Mersenne prime*, here n also is necessarily a prime number. They are named after Marin Mersenne (1588–1648), a French scientist and mathematician. In 1644, Mersenne proposed a tentative list of the powers of 2, which follow a prime number. The list included the powers, $n = 2, 3, 5, 7, 13, 17, 19, 31, 67, 127$ and 257. Over the years it has been found that Mersenne was wrong about 5 of the primes of the form—two that did not lead to a prime (67 and 257) and missed 3 that did (61, 89, 107). Following is the more recent list of exponents, n, which are the 47 Mersenne primes known till June 2009.

$$2, 3, 5, 7, 13, 17, 19, 31, 61, 89, 107, 127, 521, 607, 1279, 2203, 2281, 3217, 4253, 4423, 9689, 9941, 11213, 19937, 21701, 23209, 44497, 86243, 110503, 132049, 216091, 756839, 859433, 1257787, 1398269, 2976221, 3021377, 6972593, 13466917, 20996011, 24036583, 25964951, 30402457, 32582657, 43112609, 37156667, 42643801$$

But what is so fascinating about primes? I could not really find an answer despite consulting several mathematicians, but yes some kind of divine experience is associated with primes.

Paul Erdös one of the most prolific writers of mathematical papers, said '*God may not play dice with the universe, but something strange is going on with the prime numbers.*' Someone once said that the search for primes is like landing on the moon. It may have no real significance, but the offshoots of the technology involved are of great utility to humanity. In the search for primes, giants such as Euclid, Euler and Fermat, left in their wake, some of the greatest theorems of elementary number theory. Much of elementary number theory was developed while deciding how to handle large numbers, characterise their factors and discover those which are prime.

People love to collect beautiful and antique items. The mathematics lover would like to attach one's name to a prime number. Their greatest contribution is to the curiosity and spirit of humankind. This search also has big money involved—there are prizes for the first proved ten-million digit prime ($100000), the first hundred-million digit prime ($150000), and the first billion digit prime ($250000). Those interested can rise to the occasion and log on to *www.mersenne.org*.

Here are some interesting facts about prime numbers.

1. *A prime twin* is a pair of primes that differ by 2. Examples for prime twins are: (3, 5), (11, 13), and (1000000007, 1000000009). The largest known prime twin is

   $$242206083 \times 2^{38880} \pm 1.$$

2. Each member of this twin comprises 11,713 decimal digits!

3. Prime number 41 has an interesting property.

   41 is a prime number.

   Add 2: to get 43 which is prime

   Add 4: to get 47 prime

   Add 6: to get 53 prime

   Add 8: to get 61 prime

   Is it true for all values—can we keep adding multiples of 2 and get new primes? One can patiently try, but the fact is that it works till 41^2, after which it fails to produce a prime.

   Here is another nice one. Let us assign the value 1 to A, 2 to B, 3 to C, . . . , 26 to Z. Then

$$P + R + I + M + E = 16 + 18 + 9 + 13 + 5 = 61$$

which is a prime number.

The number 12345678901234567891 using all the 10 digits is a prime. The two numbers, 1234567891234567891234567891 and 1234567891, using only the nine digits from 1 to 9 are also prime.

4. There is also something very interesting about the number 39.

$$39 = 3 \times 13 = 3 + 5 + 7 + 11 + 13$$

As you can see, it is the product of two primes and the sum of a sequence of consecutive primes between these two primes i.e., 3 and 13.

5. After 39, there are three more such numbers: 155, 371 and 454539357304421. Even 10 has this property.

$$10 = 2 \times 5 = 2 + 3 + 5$$

Observe the table below, all the numbers are prime and have consecutive gaps.

Gap	Prime
	113575727
2	113575729
4	113575733
6	113575739
8	113575747
10	113575757
12	113575769
14	113575783
16	113575799

47

Truncating Primes

There are a few primes which are so obsessed with remaining primes that even after chopping off their last digits, they remain primes.

Here is an interesting prime number—593993. Strangely, successively truncating (*removing the last digit*) this number, we find that we are left with

59399   5939   593   59   5

which are all prime numbers. Very fascinating!

The following numbers have the same property.

73939133   23399339   29399999   37337999   59393339

When we speak of primes, we come across an interesting number sequence.

31
331
3331
33331
333331
3333331
33333331

These are all primes. Does the next number in the series 33,33,33,331 also follow the rule?

It has been found that 17 × 1,96,07,843 = 33,33,33,331. So, I suppose the series stops at where it is now. In any case, prime numbers are truly the most fascinating aspect of numbers.

48

Why are there 360° in a Circle?

Surely, you must have wondered why 360 degrees, *of all the numbers there are,* make a circle. I did some research and found that the idea originated from the Babylonians—probably due to the number system they used as well as their astronomical observation.

With the knowledge that there were approximately 360 days in a year, the Babylonian astronomers noticed that polar stars, which circle the pole everyday, seem to advance in that circle by one measure every day i.e., 1/360th of a circle. So it was natural for them to choose 360 as the number of parts of a circle.

This choice must have been further rationalised by the fact that they followed a base 60 number system. To measure a circle, a chord equal to its radius marked on the circumference would have made a natural choice of a unit. Using their sexagesimal division, they would have then taken 1/60th of this chord as the meaure i.e., one degree. They could then easily have constructed an equilateral triangle (using the chord and the radius as two sides) and discovered that whatever may be the units, there are exactly 6 equilateral triangles in a complete circle (the circle, of course, circumscribing the triangles). Thus we have $6 \times 60, 360$ degrees in a circle.

If you notice the figure, the 6 triangles also form a hexagon—the Babylonian's base system.

49

The Platonic Solids

Regular solids—geometric solids whose faces are all identical, regular polygons meeting at the same three-dimensional angles—have been a subject of intrigue and mystery to all. Their aesthetic beauty and symmetry have enchanted humans for ages. In fact, they feature prominently in Plato's philosophy. Plato believed that the universe was made of five elements and he assigned a particular regular solid to each element. The five solids were the tetrahedron (or pyramid), the cube, the octahedron, the dodecahedron, and the icosahedron.

The tetrahedron, with its sharp points and edges, was assigned to the element fire; the cube, with its four-square regularity, to earth; and the other solids invented from triangles (the octahedron and the icosahedron) to air and water, respectively. The one remaining regular solid, the dodecahedron, with 12 pentagonal faces, was assigned by Plato to the heavens with its 12 constellations. Because of Plato's development of a theory of the elements of universe based on the five regular solids, they became known as the *platonic solids*.

Kepler attempted to use the five platonic solids to help explain his model of the cosmos containing the six planets known at that time (Figure 49.1). He set the five solids one inside the other separated by a series of inscribed and circumscribed spheres, thus forming six layers corresponding to the six known planets—Mercury, Venus, Earth, Mars, Jupiter and Saturn. Based on the order (octahedron, icosahedron, dodecahedron, tetrahedron, cube), the solids could be placed at intervals corresponding relatively to the size of the planet's orbits. Thus, the cube stands between the shells of Saturn and Jupiter, the tetrahedron between those of Jupiter and Mars, and so on.

Figure 49.1 *Kepler's platonic model of the solar system*

Kepler later abandoned this model because it was not precise enough.

Now if we are looking for a formal definition of a platonic solid, it would be a polyhedron all of whose faces are congruent regular polygons, and where the same number of faces meet at every vertex. The best know example is a cube (or hexahedron) whose faces are six congruent squares. The basic polygons—triangle, square, pentagon—are used for forming the solids. This is how.

Triangles

The interior angle of an equilateral triangle is 60 degrees.

> When 3 triangles meet at each vertex, it gives rise to a tetrahedron.
>
> When 4 triangles meet at each vertex, it gives rise to an octahedron.
>
> When 5 triangles meet at each vertex, it gives rise to an icosahedron.

Squares

Since the interior angle of a square is 90 degrees, at most three squares can meet at a vertex. This is indeed possible and it gives rise to a hexahedron or cube.

Pentagons

As in the case of cubes, the only possibility is that three pentagons meet at a vertex. This gives rise to a dodecahedron.

Hexagons or regular polygons with more than six sides cannot form the faces of a regular polyhedron since their interior angles are at least 120°, and the special condition is not fulfilled. The special condition is that the interior angles of the polygons meeting at a vertex of a polyhedron should add up to *less than 360 degrees*.

Figure 49.2 shows the expansion of the solid on the right side. The tetrahedron, or pyramid (with 4 triangular faces); the cube (with 6 square faces); the octahedron (with 8 equilateral triangular faces); the dodecahedron (with 12 pentagonal faces); and the icosahedron (with 20 equilateral triangular faces).

All the platonic solids possess three concentric spheres:

the circumscribed sphere which passes through all the vertices,

the midsphere which is tangent to each edge at the midpoint of the edge, and

the inscribed sphere which is tangent to each face at the centre of the face.

Platonic solids are intimately connected with the golden section. Their striking beauty is derived from the symmetries and equalities in their relations. The symmetry of the platonic solids reveals quite appealing properties.

For instance, the cube and the octahedron both have 12 edges, but the numbers of their faces and vertices are interchanged (cube: 6

faces and 8 vertices; octahedron: 8 faces and 6 vertices). Similarly, the dodecahedron and the icosahedron both have 30 edges, but the dodecahedron has 12 faces and 20 vertices, while for the icosahedron, it is the other way round. This allows one solid to be mapped into its dual or reciprocal solid.

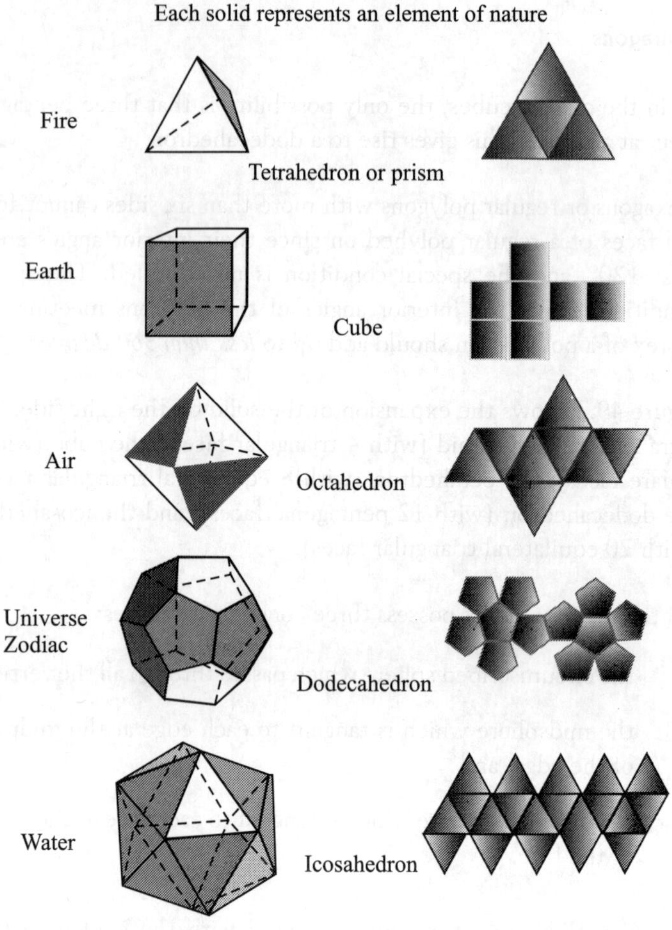

Figure 49.2 *Platonic solids*

If we connect the *centres of all the faces of a cube*, we obtain an *octahedron*, and if we connect the *centres of the faces of an octahedron*, we obtain a cube. An icosahedron can be formed similarly from a dodecahedron, and vice versa. The tetrahedron has a self-dual nature—*joining the four centres of its faces produces another inverted tetrahedron.*

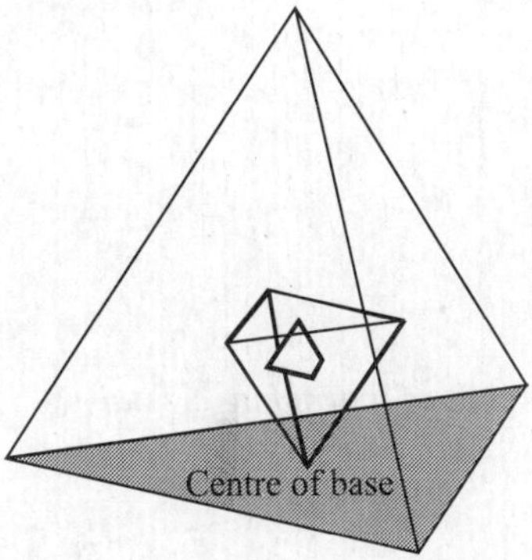

Figure 49.3 *Self-dual nature of a tetrahedron: The four centres of the faces when joined form an inverted tetrahedron*

Interestingly in Hindu mythology, the icosahedron represents *purusha*, the male, spiritual principle, which generates the dodecahedron, representing *prakriti*, the female, material principle.

The properties of the five regular polyhedra are often found in natures cycles. The platonic solids (especially the tetrahedron, octahedron, and cube) form the basis for the orderly arrangement of atoms in crystals, though the *regular* dodecahedron and icosahedron are never found. Tetrahedral geometry commonly occurs in organic and inorganic chemistry and in sub-microscopic structures. For example, the methane molecule (CH_4) is a tetrahedron, with a carbon atom at its centre and a hydrogen atom at each of its four corners.

Carbon exists in three pure forms. In graphite crystals (Figure 49.4), the carbon atoms lie in hexagonal sheets, which readily slide off a pencil as we write.

In diamond, the hardest substance known, each carbon atom is bonded to four others in a tetrahedral arrangement (Figure 49.5).

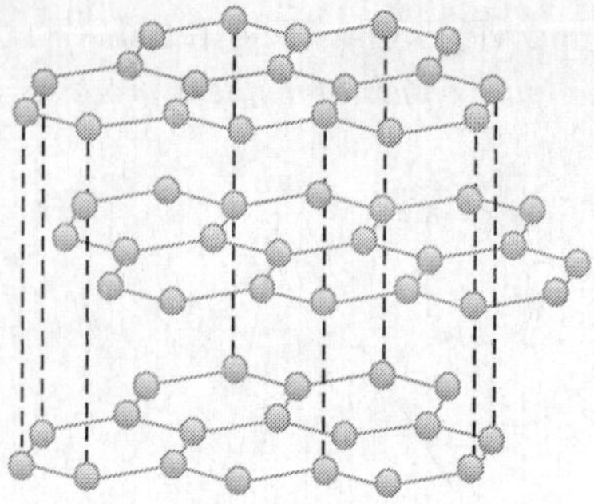

Figure 49.4 *Structure of a graphite crystal*

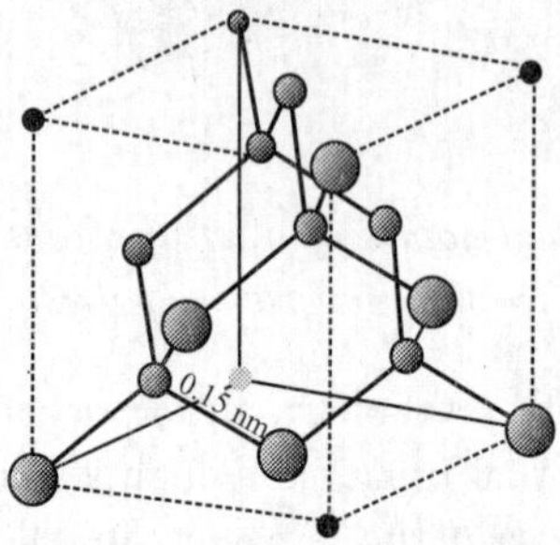

Figure 49.5 *Structure of a diamond crystal*

Buckminsterfullerene, the third, highly stable allotrope of carbon, consists of 60 carbon atoms, arranged at the vertices of a truncated icosahedron (i.e., one with its corners cut off). This is shown in Figure 49.6.

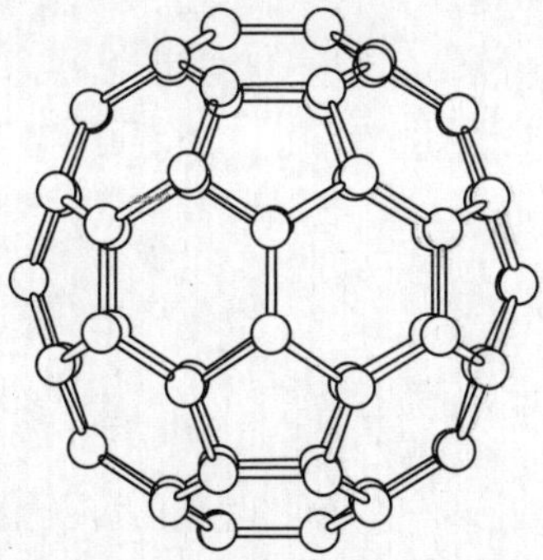

Figure 49.6 *Structure of a Buckminsterfullerene*

The great majority of viruses are icosahedral in structure, including the polio virus and the 200 kinds of viruses responsible for the common cold. Icosahedral symmetry is believed to allow for the lowest-energy configuration of particles interacting on the surface of a sphere. The five platonic solids are also found in radiolarian (radiolaria are minute protozea) skeletons.

50

Magic Squares

A 'magic square' is a rectangular array of numbers, whose each column, row, and both diagonals have the same sum.

Historically, magic squares seem to generate awe and mysticism even among great mathematicians. The history of magic squares dates back to 1000 BCE in China. A Chinese book called *Lo Shu* (book of the River Lo) relates the story of how a magic square on the back of a turtle saved the city built near Lo. By the second century BCE, there were 4 ×4 magic squares appearing, often in connection with religious practices. The Islamic/Arab mathematicians were introduced to the magic square by Indians. They then developed squares of higher order.

Here are some curious and unusual kinds of magic squares.

The Kurchan array

1037956284	1036947285	1027856394	1026847395
1026857394	1027846395	1036957284	1037946285
1036847295	1037856294	1026947385	1027956384
1027946385	1026957384	1037846295	1036857294

This amazing magic square is called the Kurchan array after its inventor. The special feature of this magic square is that all the terms are *pan-digital* i.e., all the ten digits are used without 0 being the leading digit. The magic sum is 4129607358, which again contains all the ten digits.

The apocalyptic magic square

3	107	5	131	109	311
7	331	193	11	83	41
103	53	71	89	151	199
113	61	97	197	167	31
367	13	173	59	17	37
73	101	127	179	139	47

Each row, column and diagonal of this magic square sums up to 666, the number of the beast. And incredibly all the entries are primes.

Benjamin Franklin's most amazing magic square

52	61	4	13	20	29	36	45
14	3	62	51	46	35	30	19
53	60	5	12	21	28	37	44
11	6	59	54	43	38	27	22
55	58	7	10	23	26	39	42
9	8	57	56	41	40	25	24
50	63	2	15	18	31	34	47
16	1	64	49	48	33	32	17

The magic sum for this square is 260. The most amazing thing is that all broken diagonals sum up to 260. Add up any of the marked (same shade of gray) diagonals and we will get 260.

Another interesting thing about this square is that all the half rows and columns sum up to 130. For example, consider the first half column on the left:

$52 + 14 + 53 + 11 = 130$, check it up.

Mirror magic square

96	64	37	45
39	43	98	62
84	76	25	57
23	59	82	78

This magic square has an extremely unique and miraculous property of having the magic sum of 242 for its mirror image also, which is depicted next.

69	46	73	54
93	34	89	26
48	67	52	75
32	95	28	87

Mirror square

Truly amazing!!

Multi-concentric magic square

The multi-concentric magic square of order 10 shown in this section has the magic sum of 505.

The inlaid square with 8 rows and columns has a magic sum of 404, and the inlaid square with 4 rows and columns has a magic sum of 202.

These are all pan-diagonal magic squares, which means that all the diagonals also sum up to the magic sum.

1	98	97	96	95	90	7	9	10	2
17	63	46	53	40	65	44	51	42	84
14	67	26	81	28	69	24	79	30	87
18	49	60	35	58	47	62	37	56	83
8	21	72	31	78	19	74	33	76	93
88	64	45	54	39	66	43	52	41	13
85	68	25	82	27	70	23	80	29	16
89	50	59	36	57	48	61	38	55	12
86	22	71	32	77	20	73	34	75	15
99	3	4	5	6	11	94	92	91	100

Dürer's magic square

16	3	2	13
5	10	11	8
9	6	7	12
4	15	14	1

This is probably one of the most famous magic squares ever known. It was used in an engraving entitled *Melancholia* I by Albrecht Dürer. The magic square is located on the right-hand upper corner of the engraving. The numbers 15 and 14 appear in the middle of the bottom row and indicate 1514, the year of engraving.

Melancholia I with the magic square at the right-hand upper corner

The magic sum is 34, all rows, columns and diagonals sum to 34. The most magical aspect is that all quadrants of the square also sum up to 34.

$$16+5+3+10 = 9+4+6+15 = 2+11+13+8 = 7+14+12+1$$

Moreover the middle 4 numbers add up to 34,

$$\{10+6+11+7\}$$

Any pair of numbers placed symmetrical to the centre of the square sums to 17. This is what makes it even more magical!

$$10+7, 11+6, 16+1, 13+4, 14+3, 15+2$$

51

Almost Integers

During the reader's foray into the world of mathematics and maybe even in this book, he/she might have come across numbers which are irrational, transcendental, cannot be expressed as a fraction etc., etc. Interestingly, there are some unique expressions which are almost integers using such expressions and numbers.

$\sin(11) = -0.999990206\ldots$ (in radians)

Amazing, almost 1!

These expressions involving e and π are indeed startling,

$e^{\pi} - \pi = 19.999099979\ldots$ almost 20

$e^{6} - \pi^{4} - \pi^{5} = 0.000017673\ldots$ almost 0

$\frac{\pi^{9}}{e^{8}} = 9.9998387\ldots$ almost 10

$e^{\pi\sqrt{163}} = 262537412640768743.99999999999992500\ldots$

$e^{\pi\sqrt{58}} = 24591257751.9999998222\ldots\ldots$

$e^{\pi\sqrt{37}} = 199148647.99997804\ldots\ldots$

$e^{\pi\sqrt{22}} = 2508951.998257\ldots\ldots$

All of them are so close to an integer!

A few more almost integers become so in the following manner,

Raising π to the fourth power, we get

$$22\pi^4 = 2143.000002748\ldots$$

Following are a few expressions using logarithms

$$510\log_{10} 7 = 431.00000040\ldots$$

$$88\ln 89 = 395.00000053\ldots$$

$$272\log_\pi 97 = 1087.000000204$$

$$\frac{163}{\ln 163} = 31.9999987384\ldots$$

$$\frac{53453}{\ln 53453} = 4910.00000122\ldots$$

Some expressions are very, very close to being integers,

$$\left(\frac{23}{9}\right)^5 = \frac{6436343}{59049} = 109.00003387\ldots$$

$$3\sqrt{2}(\sqrt{5}-2) = 1.0015516\ldots$$

$$\frac{1}{3^{1/3}\ln 2} = 1.00030887\ldots$$

With just e, we have the following expression: $\frac{613}{37}e - \frac{35}{991} = 44.999999999$

There is also an expression using the golden ratio and ln 2

$$\frac{\varphi}{2^{\ln 2}} = 1.0007590\ldots$$

This chapter is adapted from Eric W. Weisstein's article 'Almost Integer' available at http://mathworld.wolfram.com/AlmostInteger.html

End Note: What is Mathematics?

A mathematician is a blind man in a dark room looking for a black cat which isn't there.

Charles Darwin

What makes mathematics different from any another subject? Does being a mathematician mean that you belong to a distinct set of people? Let me start my discussion with a little story.

> An engineer, a physicist and a mathematician are all put in a room with a burning fire in the middle and one bucket of water next to it. This is how they respond:
>
> The engineer, practical as he is, takes the bucket and throws the water over the fire to put it off instantly.
>
> The physicist, curious as he is, takes the bucket and pours the water all around the fire and watches the fire die out slowly.
>
> *The mathematician walks about in the room, observes the fire and the bucket of water, thinks for a moment, determines there is a solution and leaves the room again.*

Does this explain all? An engineer thinks that his equations are an approximation to reality. A physicist thinks reality is an approximation to his equations. A pure mathematician does not care about reality—he only needs to knows that there is an abstract equation to approximate reality.

The word 'mathematics' comes from the Greek $\mu\acute{\alpha}\theta\eta\mu\alpha$ (máthema) meaning 'science, knowledge, or learning' and $\mu\alpha\theta\eta\mu\alpha\tau\iota\kappa\acute{o}\zeta$ (mathematikós) meaning 'fond of learning'. It is often abbreviated to 'maths' in Commonwealth English and 'math' in North American English. India uses the abbreviation 'maths'.

Mathematics is defined as study of quantity, structure, space and change. It is used in every society for accounting, measuring land, predicting astronomical events. The pure mathematician often does not bother about the practical application of his theory. But the remarkable thing is that it ends up in some very useful applications. This prompted physicist Eugene Wigner (1902–1995) to lecture on '*the unreasonable effectiveness of mathematics*'. Natural sciences depend heavily on new mathematical discoveries.

The elegance of mathematics is intrinsic in its simplicity and generality. There is beauty in a difficult proof, and *if the result is not beautiful it is not thought of as correct.* In *A Mathematician's Apology*, G. H. Hardy expressed the belief that aesthetic considerations in themselves are sufficient to justify the study of pure mathematics.

Writings in mathematics are not easily accessible to the layperson. This was the compromise Stephen Hawking made while writing the bestseller *A Brief History of Time*—his book had only one mathematical equation.

The mathematical notation is a very recent development (although in this book we began with this topic). Before that, mathematics was written out in words, resulting in lengthy and cumbersome texts. Now a few symbols are enough to convey a whole lot of information. Common words like 'and', 'or', 'only' have very precise meanings in mathematics.

There is an ongoing debate, quite unnecessary I feel, on the qualification of mathematics as a science. Gauss called mathematics the Queen of Sciences. But if one considers science as being strictly of the natural world, then one cannot consider pure mathematics as a science. Some theorists also claim that mathematics is not experimentally falsifiable (it cannot be shown to be false or true by an observation or physical experiment). But I believe that similar to all other fields of science, mathematics relies on intuition and experimentation. Since many mathematical conjectures are formed out of experimentation, mathematics can be labelled as a science.

Major disciplines within mathematics arose out of the inevitable need for calculations in commerce, understanding relationships between numbers and most importantly, predicting astronomical events for the purposes of astrology. This perhaps is the one of greatest offshoot advantages of astrology—that its believers forced the development of mathematics. Thus, four main fields, *arithmetic, algebra, geometry* and *analysis (calculus)*, matured simultaneously complementing each other.

Arithmetic concerns itself with the study of quantity, starting with numbers and arithmetical operators. The higher properties are studied in number theory. Algebra is plainly a study of structures. It led to abstract numbers such as the square root of 2. The concept of vectors, groups, rings, fields etc. are all developments of algebra. The study of space originates with geometry. It has offshoots like trigonometry, analytic geometry, topology, differential geometry, combining concepts of quantity and space. Calculus was developed as a tool for understanding and describing change. The relationship of quantity and rate of change is differential calculus. An important field in applied mathematics is statistics whose basis is probability theory. Its greatest tool, numerical analysis, takes a broad range of mathematical problems which are otherwise beyond human capacity and simplifies them for computers to solve.

I would like to recite one more story to show the famed impractical nature of the common mathematician.

The mathematician Mr Math, had to move to a new place. His wife did not trust him very much when dealing with practical issues like getting transport. So when they stood down on the street with all their things around them, she asked him to watch their ten trunks, while she got a taxi. Some minutes later she returned.

Said the husband, 'I thought you said there were ten trunks, but I've only counted to nine.'

The wife said: 'No, there are TEN!'

Replied he, '*But I have counted them: 0, 1, 2, . . .*'

But jokes apart, essentially mathematics is nothing more than the language of science. While science is a systematic study of nature, mathematics is a concise form of communication used to represent nature. Russians so believed that mathematics was the language of the Universe that the message they wanted to send out to living beings in outer space was

$$10^2 + 11^2 + 12^2 = 13^2 + 14^2$$

Both the sides of the equation add up to 365—the numbers of days in a year.

There are facets of mathematics, which are bewildering and seem quite unnatural—they seem more like forcefully finding patterns when there is seemingly no symmetry. But that's the fun of abstraction—the license to simply *generalise*.

Books to Read

1. Aczel, Amir. 1996. *Fermat's Last Theorem.* New York: Bantam Dell Books. *A history and mathematical discussion of Fermat's Last Theorem as studied over the centuries, culminating in its solution by Andrew Wiles.*

2. Blatner, David. 1997. *The Joy of Pi.* Birmingham: Walker Publishing. *This is a very nice account of the history and culture of pi.*

3. Clawson, Calvin. 1996. *Mathematical Mysteries: The Beauty and Magic of Numbers.* New York: Plenum Publishing. *A very well-written introduction to number theory.*

4. Boyer, Carl. 1968. *A History of Mathematics*. New Jersey: John Wiley Publishing. *This is a classic textbook on the history of mathematics.*

5. Casti, John. 1996. *Five Golden Rules: Great Theories of 20th Mathematics – and Why They Matter*. New Jersey: John Wiley Publishing. *This gives an intelligent and readable discussion of some great mathematical ideas of this century, with applications of those ideas outside of mathematics.*

6. Conway, John and Richard Guy. 1996. *The Book of Numbers.* New York: Springer-Verlag. *An interesting presentation and discussion of numbers, from integers to the hyper-reals.*

7. Courant, Richard and Herbert Robbins; revised by Ian Stewart. 1996. *What is Mathematics?* Oxford: Oxford University Press. *This is an update of a classic introduction to mathematics.*

8. Davis, Philip. 1983. *The Thread: A Mathematical Yarn.* Sussex: Harvester Press. *This is a unique and eclectic tale tying together mathematical ideas and personalities across the centuries. An interesting and enjoyable read!*

9. Davis, Philip and Reuben Hersh. 1981. *The Mathematical Experience.* Basel: Birkhäuser Publishing. *This is a very readable account, incorporating discussions of the major areas of mathematics and the history of mathematics.*

10. Dörrie, Heinrich. 1965. *100 Great Problems of Elementary Mathematics: Their History and Solution.* New York: Dover Publications. *This is an English language translation of the original German text published in 1958. A book of very interesting solutions, a must for any maths lover.*

11. Edwards, Jr., C. H. 1979. *The Historical Development of the Calculus.* New York: Springer-Verlag.

12. Fadiman, Clifton. 1997. *Fantasia Mathematica.* New York: Springer-Verlag. *Reprint from the 1958 publication: A collection of miscellaneous stories and other materials involving mathematics.*

13. Gleick, James. 1987. *Chaos: Making a New Science.* New York: Penguin Books. *This is a very well-read popular account of chaos theory and the associated topics of dynamical systems and fractal geometry.*

14. Hardy, G. H. 1940. *A Mathematician's Apology* (with a forward by C. P. Snow). Cambridge: Cambridge University Press. *This is a personal (and very famous) account of doing mathematics by a 'mathematical great'* .

15. Hoffman, Paul. 1999. *The Man Who Loved Only Numbers.* London: Fourth Estate Limited. *This is a biography of Paul Erds, a great mathematician of the 20th century.*

16. Hodges, Andrew. 1983. *Alan Turing: The Enigma. New York:* Simon & Schuster. *This is a biography of one of the most important deep thinkers in the development of modern computing, a man whose name is given to the premier award in computer science, The Turing Award.*

17. Joseph, George Gheverghese. 1992. *The Crest of the Peacock: Non-European Roots of Mathematics.* New York: Penguin Books. *This is an excellent source of history on the contributions to the development of mathematics from ancient Egypt, Babylonia, India, China, the Arab world, and other parts of the non-European world.*

18. Körner, T. W. 1996. *The Pleasures of Counting.* Cambridge: Cambridge University Press. *A well-written and interesting introductory discussion of many areas of mathematics.*

19. Lakoff, George and Rafael Núñez. 2000. *Where Mathematics Comes From: How The Embodied Mind Brings Mathematics Into Being.* New York: Basic Books. *This is a cognitive analysis of the structure of mathematical ideas.*

20. Maor, Eli. 1994. *e: The Story of a Number.* Princeton: Princeton University Press. *This is a history of the number e, discussing also the history of pi, i, and other important quantities in mathematics.*

21. Needham, Tristan. 1997. *Visual Complex Analysis.* Gloucestershire: Clarendon Press, 1997. *This is a lovely presentation of complex analysis, emphasising its geometric connections.*

22. Peterson, Ivars. 1988. *The Mathematical Tourist: Snapshots of Modern Mathematics.* Virginia: Freeman Publishers.

23. Seife, Charles. 2000. *Zero: The Biography of a Dangerous Idea.* New York: Penguin Books. *This is a historical and mathematical analysis of the development of the idea of zero in our number system, explaining its historical significance outside of mathematics, especially in religion and philosophy.*

24. Simmons, George. 1992. *Calculus Gems: Brief Lives and Memorable Mathematics.* Ohio: McGraw-Hill Publishing. *An account of the major figures in the development of calculus, together with a discussion on some of the important mathematical problems studied in this development.*

25. Smith, David. 1959. *A Source Book in Mathematics.* New York: Dover Publications. *This was originally published in*

1929, and it contains original writings from important papers of well-known mathematicians from 1478 onwards.

26. Stewart, Ian. 1987. *The Problems of Mathematics.* Oxford: Oxford Press. *It discusses the 'nature of mathematics' by looking at particular important problems, many of interest in current applications to real-world problems (e.g. cryptology). Stewart is one of best known popularisers of mathematics.*

27. Stewart, Ian. 1989. *Does God Play Dice? The Mathematics of Chaos.* Oxford: Blackwell Publishers. *A very readable account of chaos theory and the associated topics of dynamical systems and fractal geometry.*

28. Stewart, Ian. 1995. *Nature's Numbers: The Unreal Reality of Mathematics.* New York: Basic Books.

29. Stillwell, John. 1989. *Mathematics and Its History.* New York: Springer-Verlag.

30. Stewart, Ian. 1989. *Game, Set, and Math: Enigmas and Conundrums.* Cambridge: Basil Blackwell.

31. Dudeney, Henry E. 1958. *Amusements in Mathematics.* New York: Dover.

32. Dudeney, Henry E. 1958. *The Canterbury Puzzles.* New York: Dover.

33. Dudeney, Henry E. 1967. 536 *Puzzles and Curious Problems.* New York: Charles Scribner's.

34. Gardner, Martin. ed. 1959. *The Mathematical Puzzles of Sam Lloyd. 2 vols.* New York: Dover.

Mathematics on the Internet

A few of the more interesting Websites for general as well as recreational mathematics are listed below. They are listed in order of the author's preference.

1. mathworld.wolfram.com

2. www-history.mcs.st-andrews.ac.uk

3. www.cut-the-knot.org
4. mathforum.org/library
5. archives.math.utk.edu/topics
6. www.math.com
7. richardphillips.org.uk
8. www.archimedes-lab.org
9. www.worldofnumbers.com
10. www-groups.dcs.st-and.ac.uk
11. www.sunsite.ubc.ca/LivingMathematics
12. www.maa.org
13. hlavolamy.szm.sk
14. www.brainbashers.com
15. www.math.utah.edu
16. thesaurus.maths.org
17. www.lboro.ac.uk
18. www.brainteaser-world.com
19. www.math-atlas.org
20. numbers.computation.free.fr
21. aleph0.clarku.edu
22. www.mathsisfun.com
23. www.perplexus.info
24. www.stetson.edu
25. sciencegems.com/math.html#1
26. plus.maths.org

27. www.heartofmath.com

Google search reveal millions of pages on mathematics. The online encyclopedia Wikipedia, (en.wikipedia.org/wiki) has pages of interesting information and links to some of the best Websites on almost any topic in mathematics.

Index